MORE PRAISE FOR
CIRCADIAN

"I have never read an interrogation of language, gender politics, or aftermath quite like Clammer's passionately searing *Circadian*. Though evocative of writers from Anne Carson to Kate Zambreno, Clammer's urgency and electricity here create a flash of lightning all her own."

—Gina Frangello
author of *A Life of Men* and *Every Kind of Wanting*

"In these beautifully written essays, Clammer considers the intricate, confounding, and powerful connections between story and body, narrative and physical form. She examines the subject of trauma through a series of innovative frames, casting a fearless and curious gaze on her material and bringing new insights to life."

—Marya Hornbacher
New York Times bestselling author of *Wasted*

"In sharp, beautiful language, Chelsey Clammer creates elegant, intimate prose about the violence of being female, being a daughter, the way PTSD engraves itself upon us, altering us body and mind, majorly shaping our experience of our own lives. A powerful book."

—Michelle Tea
author of *Black Wave*

"Chelsey Clammer's new book of essays, *Circadian,* is a lyrical, playful, and delightfully idiosyncratic exploration of everyday wonder, language, and the 'poetics of pain.' Her voice is surefooted and smart, deftly guiding her reader through rich landscapes of memory and meaning; but it's also equally critical and confrontational, holding a light up to experiences that demand our witness and daring us to think deeply."

—Steven Church

author of *One with the Tiger*
Nonfiction Editor for *The Normal School*

CIRCADIAN

essays

CHELSEY CLAMMER

 Red Hen Press | *Pasadena, CA*

Book layout by Cassidy Trier

Library of Congress Cataloging-in-Publication Data
Names: Clammer, Chelsey, author.
Title: Circadian : essays / Chelsey clammer.
Description: First edition. | Pasadena, CA : Red Hen Press, [2017]
Identifiers: LCCN 2017011410 | ISBN 9781597096034 (pbk. : alk.
paper) | ISBN 9781597095709 (Ebook)
Classification: LCC PS3603.L348 A6 2017 | DDC 813/.6—dc23
LC record available at https://lccn.loc.gov/2017011410

The National Endowment for the Arts, the Los Angeles County
Arts Commission, the Dwight Stuart Youth Fund, the Max
Factor Family Foundation, the Pasadena Tournament of Roses
Foundation, the Pasadena Arts & Culture Commission and
the City of Pasadena Cultural Affairs Division, the City of Los
Angeles Department of Cultural Affairs, the Audrey & Sydney
Irmas Charitable Foundation, Sony Pictures Entertainment,
Amazon Literary Partnership, and the Sherwood Foundation
partially support Red Hen Press.

First Edition
Published by Red Hen Press
www.redhen.org

ACKNOWLEDGMENTS

Another Chicago Magazine: "Circadian"; *Best New Writing*: "Twenty-Six Junctures of How I Am a Part of You"; *Black Warrior Review*: "Mother Tongue"; *Essay Daily*: "Body of Work," "Lying in the Lyric," and "Trigger Happy"; *Green Mountains Review*: "Outline for Change"; *Hobart*: "Re: Collection"; *The James Franco Review*: "Then She Flew Away"; *The Lableter*: "I Could Title This Wavering"; *New Delta Review*: "On Three"; and *Water~Stone Review*: "A Striking Resemblance."

To all the strong women in my life who keep me going,
again and again.

CONTENTS

ON THREE

- In order to be considered a healthy weight, a 6'2" man should weigh between 171 and 209 pounds.
- His oak dresser weighs 209 pounds.
- He is 6'2" and 252 pounds and fifty-two years old. The dresser is in better shape than he is.
- It will take two men to move the dresser.
- It will take two men to move the dresser from a 3,128 square-foot, five-bedroom house with a three-car garage into a 26-foot truck.
- A football field is 57,600 square feet.
- 18.41 replicas of his house could fit in a football field.
- Every Sunday from early fall to mid-winter, he steers his screams to the football players on TV.
- Go Broncos.
- After his promotion, he had the 3,128 square-foot house built to his specifications for his family. Four years later and one daughter's in Houston for college, and the other one's in Georgetown for college, and he loses his job in Austin due to all of the drinking he did at his desk, and now he and his wife have to vacate the 3,128 square feet.

- In order to move a five-bedroom house, a moving company will send at least four workers to get everything loaded into their 26-foot truck within six hours. Six hours to move everything out of a five-bedroom house is plenty of time for four movers to get the job done, as long as everything goes as planned.
- "Ma'am? We have a problem in here."
- The oak dresser that is in better shape than he is, is not the problem.
- A king size mattress should be wrapped in a protective sheet of plastic before it is moved onto a truck. At least 46 square feet of plastic is needed to wrap the entire mattress. The length of the plastic is not the problem.
- An unhealthy 6'2" motionless man weighs down the mattress with his 252 pounds.
- Sales people promise a mattress will last ten years before it needs to be replaced. However, the weight of the person on the mattress, as well as the duration that person spends on it will vary this number. Indentations in the mattress can begin to appear in as little as two years.
- He lies in one of the indentations in the mattress, one of the two dips that prove he does not touch his wife at night, that she does not touch him, the separated depressions on each side of the bed like two shallow graves. His body fills the plot on the left.

- A handle of 80-proof vodka contains 3,830 calories. If one were to subsist solely on a diet of one handle of 80-proof vodka per day, and if that person were to sleep the whole day and never exercise, then that person would consume a surplus of 1,330 calories a day. At this rate, a pound would be gained every 2.71 days. That's a pound every 64.96 hours. Last night, he consumed his liquid meal for the day, and then went to sleep after the Broncos game. And now he continues to sleep. He is, in fact, entering into his sixteenth hour of sleep, which means one quarter of a pound has already been added to the 252.
- "Ma'am? We have a problem in here."
- In order for a person to hear you speak clearly from 20 feet away, your voice needs to be projected at the force of 60 decibels.
- The movers stand 10 feet away from his bed. It is not he who responds to their 60 decibels, but his wife. She is 30 feet away from them and behind two sets of walls as she packs up the Fiestaware in the kitchen. Their voices are a whisper, but she still hears them, or rather senses the sound of desperation brewing in the master bedroom down the hall.
- The movers look at him, at each other, at the wife as she enters the room, arms immediately crossing her chest. He is a problem she does not know how to solve.

- Wuzzle: word puzzle consisting of combinations of words and letters to create disguised words or phrases.
- As in: NOONGOOD = Good afternoon.
- As in:

> G
> MORNING
>   I
>   T
>   T
>   E
>   G

- There is no getting up in this morning.
- A fifty-two-year-old businessman with no college degree who is fired because he drinks on the job possibly does not know how to solve the problem, either. Perhaps he doesn't care to. Perhaps his life is a concept he will never get.
- "Jeff?"
- It takes the brain 0.013 seconds to understand an image the eyes see.
- She stares at him as he continues to lie, conked out, the 3,830 calories of 80-proof vodka weighing his body down.
- He was sober for thirteen years. That's 676 Mondays of sobriety.
- It is eleven o'clock on a Monday morning.

- After this Monday, he will drink for another two years before he dies. That's 104 intoxicated Mondays. That's one final sip which will tip his blood-alcohol level to 0.46. That's 5.75 times the legal limit of 0.08. That's impressive.
- On this Monday, he does not reply to her when she says his name. The movers look at him again, at each other, at my mother.
- She sighs.
- "Just put him on the floor."
- A man who weighs 252 pounds has to steadily drink 28.5 ounces of vodka to lose consciousness. That's just under a liter of liquor. That's 19 drinks.
- I am 19 when my father doesn't move on moving day.
- The movers have 46 square feet of plastic waiting to be used.
- She sighs.
- "Just put him on the floor."
- Lift with your legs, not with your back.
- On the count of three.

MOTHER TONGUE

Idiom: "Don't eat your words."

Condition: "I can taste my words."

Diagnosis: *Lexical–Gustatory Synesthesia.*

Lexical slinks off the tongue, its sound a little creek-like, its letters slipping over the pebbles of taste buds, the liquidy linguistics that tinkle past lips.

Gustatory fills the mouth's cavern, its weight weighing down the tongue, its full, cumbersome body heaved over lips with an ungainly gush.

Synesthesia. It stutters. It lisps. Lips confused about formation, pronunciation tangled and twisted on a tongue that knows not how or when to let go.

The shape of these sounds strung awkwardly together, one after another after another and another, create a type of lingual topography—*lexical-gustatory synesthesia*—where the tongue attends to the crux of its cadences, taste buds puckering, the full menu of this phrase rolling around a mouth that wants to savor its meaning. Six courses of syllables served twice.

The salivary experience of *lexical-gustatory synesthesia* is an interesting sense to consider. Because consider this: having *lexical-gustatory synesthesia* means "clock" transmutes into licorice on the tongue. Yes, it's true. Some people have a palate for vocabulary's succulence. Some people taste words. "Chair" has a chocolate flavor. "Stop sign," macaroons. "Skyscraper" has a zest of lime. How jealous are you?

Taste and touch and reading and hearing all bleed together on the tongue. Paths crossing. Convergence. The translation of words into taste.

We all did this as children, learned the tactility and taste of words as a way to understand them, remembering the flavor of phrases to somehow get to know them. But then we grew up. The conversation between word and taste silenced with age. The flavor of language now lost.

⊢——————————⊣

I'm sitting at my grandmother's dining room table, gazing across the plateau of its weathered wood surface, staring at a certain server named Susan. She sits, looking up, wondering what she can do to please me next. Nothing. She knows this, stays still. My eyes eye the bits of her own plateau, though her weathered wood surface wears a white doily—the only outfit in her wardrobe. A uniform of sorts. White threads knitted together in a particular pattern placed on top of her, the doily lets the dark wood peek through its loopy weave. Susan and her doily have been sitting here since 1973. In the past four decades, Susan's purpose has stayed the same. Various dining table necessities sit on top of her—the expected accoutrements of salt and pepper shakers, as well as a wicker chicken circa 1970 containing small pink packets of sweetener. They have all been here since the table was first set forty years ago. Same with the woven napkin holder. The small opaque blue vase that contains a bouquet of fake baby's breath. Hovering above Susan, the amalgamation of these items' scents seep into my nose. The fragrance then cascades down the back door of my sinuses, leading to my tongue, which then interprets it as taste. The flavor of history. I reach out, spin Susan around with a soft force from my fingertips. I wonder about her lineage. I want to know what brought her here.

⊢————————————————⊣

Katrina isn't what she used to be. It used to be that Katrina was a frequently chosen name for children. At the beginning of 2005, she was the 246th most commonly used girl name on the baby name list. And then the summer came. And then a hurricane. And then 1,800 deaths. And now Katrina is no longer wanted. She's despised, feared. Or more accurately, loathed. Katrina. And how her name is a keepsake no one wants to carry. A stressor triggering traumatic memories that residents who not only remained, but survived, no longer want to recognize as a part of their pasts. The water receded as *X*'s started to arrive on every front door. The headcount of those who stayed behind, stayed inside, the ones who died, are now just part of a number spray-painted on the soggy outside walls of these ruined homes. Five. And nine over there. Here's one.

Katrina is their trauma.

Her usage declines. Recedes.

2006: 379th on the baby name list.

2010: 865th on the baby name list.

2011: She no longer exists in the top 1,000 of the baby name list. The desire for her has regressed. She hasn't been this low since 1961.

No one wants Katrina.

The power of what a name can do.

⊢―――――――――――⊣

Our server's full name is Lazy Susan, which does not fit her as she is always busy. The trait of always working. Even at a standstill, Lazy Susan doesn't neglect her duties of swiveling around to help serve those accoutrements. She creates convenience, performs her job quite well. Always has.

Give Susan a little spin, and she soon presents the blue and white bowl containing sugar, sugar that surprisingly still tastes similar to what sugar should taste like, even though it has congealed into a mountain range of saccharine over the past few decades. The contents of the blue and white bowl forgotten, but the dutiful Lazy Susan still holds them.

She made space for us, gave the basic flavors of condiment staples room to squat. Right on top of her. And the ways in which Lazy Susan revolves was revolutionary. A reinvention of tradition. Instant popularity. She was born from innovation. Lazy Susan will be remembered for centuries, though not her history. Her heritage, her origins, even the year of her birth are all forgotten. Historians long ago surrendered to the futile investigation of the origins of her name—yes, why *Susan*? Even the Smithsonian is answerless. Research never succeeded to weave together the fraying threads of her lineage.

⊢————————————⊣

The headline reads: "Dictionary Makers Kill the Cassette Player to Make Room for the Mankini."

Words eventually evaporate.

Example:

There was quite a *brabble*[1] last night over at the *growlery*.[2] Some *script kiddie*[3] was discussing the *threequel*[4] of her science fiction series about *glocalization*[5] with a friend who at one point challenged her use of a *cassette player*[6] in the opening scene. The author argued it was important in regards to the *millennium bug*[7] theme.

Eh?

―――――――――――

1. Paltry noisy quarrel.
2. Place in which to growl.
3. A person who uses existing scripts or codes to hack into computers, lacking the expertise to write their own.
4. The third film, book, event, etc. in a series; a second sequel.
5. The practice of conducting business according to both local and global considerations.
6. A machine for playing back or recording audio cassette.
7. An inability in older computing software to deal correctly with dates of January 1, 2000 or later.

2012: The *Oxford English Dictionary* declared those words no longer needed to be heard. That to define them was now unnecessary. We grow away from words. The generations of people who used them will one day die off. Vocabulary vanishes.

Nouns neglected.

Eurocommunism lost to *noob*.

Halier lost to *nurdle*.

Video jockey lost to *jeggings*.

The irrelevance of a phrase. Once unwanted, prose departs. But who decides when language dies?

⊢————————————⊣

Throws like a girl. Cries like a bitch. Nervous as a whore in church. Drier than a nun's nasty. Bitch-slapped. Momma's boy. Bookslut. Chick flick. Chick lit. Debbie Downer. Titty-bong. That was a bitch. Son of a bitch. Sweats like a blind dyke in a fish market. Bimbo. Fag Hag. Pussy. Pussy-whipped. Mother fucker. Fucking cunt. Prima donna. Cold as a witch's tit. Whines like a little bitch.

⊢————————————⊣

I'm five years old and I'm still trying to figure out the concept of correct pronunciation.

"Mom, I want ice cweam."

"Look, Mom! The's a wainbow!"

Enter: speech therapist. My mother wants my mouth to act normal, wants my tongue to be able to handle the alphabet, lips moving like lips are supposed to move for each letter, each word. I won't remember the speech lessons, but I will remember the feel of the misplaced *W* in my mouth, the way it weighs down my tongue, the cushiony taste to it. Wedding cake. *W* is richer, a more full-mouth sense than the stark *R*. Rice cake.

The tongue tastes. The tongue speaks, forming words that started out as a silent idea. Lips lining the mouth are good for keeping food in. Lips lining the mouth are also good for guiding each word out (of the way). And then there's the teeth. Teeth controlling the latitude of language, conducting air as it flows from esophagus to mouth. And then out. The bite at the end of a sentence. And the tongue follows, strikes the teeth, lashes, clashes with it to complete a sound that holds meaning. And then that one final push to bring the word out, to transform air into sound, to vocalize what's inside so I can connect with you, out here. Converse. The air that attends to us both.

And yet. At times, words protest the mouth. Stuck in that space between brain and air. A holding cell. Lodged. A type of _____. Um, a type of _____. Hmm, a type of _____. Well shit. A type of _____. Damn. What's the word I'm looking for? It's right on the tip of my tongue.

├───────────────────┤

In regards to the Lazy Susan's history there are a few knowns.

1313: Author Wang Zhen pioneered a moveable table whose surface consisted of 1,000 organized Chinese characters. The table spun and moved, relieving the typesetter of the constant, monotonous movements of repositioning his body to be able to reach each one of the 1,000 characters.

600 years go by.

1917: Dr. Wu Lien-Teh believed communal Chinese meals were a hotbed of disease. Enter: "hygienic dining tray" with its swiveling capabilities and serving spoons and separate chopsticks. He traveled all over China to see if anyone had already invented a rotating tray. He found nothing that resembled his idea.

35 years go by.

1953: Johnny Kan opens a Cantonese-style restaurant in San Francisco. He has two Chinese-American buddies who help him out, one of whom is George Hall. George starts tinkering around with wood and ball bearings until one day his tinkering stops. He has completed his invention. The revolving table was born (again?) and would become a pivotal facet of Johnny's new banquet room. The Lazy Susan (re: *how "Susan"?* re: *why "Susan"?* Certainly she wasn't Chinese) would become a household name, would transform the once-cramped and dingy Chinese tables into refined and spacious eating arrangements.

Popularity exploded.

And then a few years go by.

1960: The Lazy Susan becomes a standard fare, as common as Fiestaware.

54 years go by.

2014: I return to my grandmother's house during my winter vacation, and I spot the Lazy Susan still on her dinner table. I become curious out of boredom. Susan, where did you come from?

I do some cursory research. Wikipedia doesn't know. Ask. com doesn't have an answer. Google is clueless. Again, even the Smithsonian has surrendered, has said they can't discern the why and the how of "Lazy Susan."

No one knows for sure Susan's history. Something is lost.

Her heritage is apparently not important enough to remember. The Lazy Susan is proof that history can be deleted, forgotten. Can disappear. A lineage silenced. No one seems to care. No one finds the history, the meaning of her name necessary to know.

Let's say the doctor was right. Let's say my mother's assumptions were right. Let's say the old wives' tale is true.

If they had all been correct, if my strong heartbeat and high placement in the womb did indeed indicate I was a boy, then I would have been beat up each day of my childhood, if not my entire life.

Thank god I was born penis-less, because if I hadn't my name would be Cosmo.

Cosmo Clammer. Destined to be taunted. Doomed to be despised. No one would have cared my name meant *order*, meant *harmony*, meant *beauty*. No, the ugly, clunky sound of Cosmo Clammer uncontrollably cartwheels out of your mouth like vomit. And an inevitable insult would surely have been hurled after it. Every time. Taunts spewed.

Let's look at statistics.

Statistically speaking, Cosmo is not a well-received name in any era, any decade.

57,870 out of 88,799 on the list of preferred names for baby boys.

Mom, seriously?

That's 500 lexicon points automatically deducted for even considering *Cosmo.*

About lexicon points.

My friend and I track our lexical scores.

It works like this:

Come up with a new word that is as witty as it is perfect for the situation it describes.

Recognize the inventive linguistics and scream "lexicon point!"

Such as:

"Hippies living in Texas? Those *dreadnecks!*"

"Lexicon point!"

"That dyke's dating a dude now? What a *hasbian!*"

"Lexicon point!"

"Did you see her girlfriend? They look like twins! Such *dopplebangers!*"

"Lexicon point!"

"Dang. All that fucking last night made me sore. I have a total *bangover*!"

"Lexicon point!"

From these provided examples, I see that

a) it's completely obvious my friend and I are queer.

b) three out of our favorite top four lexicon points are in reference to something sex-related.

c) *lexicon point* might be the wrong phrase for this section.

d) perhaps *sexicon point* is what we live for.[8]

"Good god that woman knows what she's doing. She's a fucking *cunt connoisseur*!"

"Sexicon point!"

New words ripple from our tongues, followed by that feeling of power, of claiming, of making, of changing our engagement with language. Wrapping new words around each other, cinching our identities, putting them in sync with one another. It's more than a friendship with words. It's love. A lovership with language.

<3

But not all language is loved. Declaring progress is a questionable practice. We've gone from *fob* to *immigrant*. Changed *secretary* to *administrative assistant*. Being *retarded* is now hav-

---

8. Lexicon point!

ing a *cognitive disability*. *Crazy* is just a *mental illness*, if not a *mental health issue*. But command of language ≠ control over things to be filed under "Up, Fucked." Poetry can't turn *fugly* into *pretty* because some socially constructed conceptions resist reformation. Some words, some phrases just won't go away, no matter how much they are hated by how many. They're so soaked in our history, planted in our mouths that unthinkingly speak them. Racist phrases we rely on. My sister laughs at how I nigger-rigged my car's engine with a sock. Mom thinks my aunt is an Indian giver. My friend thinks her cousin is a porch monkey. I get annoyed when she nigger-lips the cigarette we're sharing. And Grandma asks me if I'm out of my cotton-pickin' mind.

Also, the full-bodied taste of full-body hatred that resonates in her mouth with an intense, rich flavor of restriction.

Yes, a woman's mouth must cease movement to obtain the unattainable standards of female flesh.

If not eating, then what?

Swish then spit.

If her mouth is not empty, then it should be full of him. So says misogyny. It's the way it's always been and the way it will always be. She is here to please.

According to sexism, according to misogyny, a woman's mouth has two positions: the money shot's *O*, or lips closed. Either way, a woman chokes on silence. Swallow that. An old-school sexist standard of purpose, of *beauty* is still taught to young girls today.

It's elementary, really.

Let's calculate the age of this type of oppression.

The answer is easy.

The oppression of 0's. As in, her clothes. The body she's supposed to have, the body that a sexist society says he owns. Her mouth will never learn the pleasure of eating. No need to know, really. Her throat is meant to be closed. Less is more. He approves of her open *O*.

⊢————————————⊣

The black-eyed Susan.

Oh Susan, what'd you do? If you stopped being so lazy he wouldn't punch you.

⊢————————————⊣

Grandma sits across the kitchen table from me and speaks of her husband as if he is alive.

"Well," my grandmother says as she spins her Lazy Susan around with the soft force of her knobby fingers, "your granddad says you can only be happy if you love your family."

Granddad died three years ago.

Her verb is misused.

No matter.

Because her language keeps Granddad alive, revitalizing his memory to ward him away from historylessness.

(Lexicon point)

———————————

We can't ignore the lexicon we loathe, would love for the *OED* to declare dead.

We fight to forget, try to set forth on setting right the reverberations of the lexically oppressive.

We try to fix it.

Here, this might help:

1956: Bette Graham is transcribing her boss's letter on a typewriter. She accidently hits *G* instead of *H*, and when she goes to erase it, the ink smears. This looks unprofessional. So she gets a tidbit of paint from the cabinet, tinkers around with its color to match the hue of her stationary, and, well look at that: a fixed mistake.

The idea catches on. Everyone wants this *miracle masking mixture*, as they call it. So in her home Bette starts making batches of her "Mistake-Out."

23 years go by.

1979: Bette sells her business to the Gillette Corporation for $47.5 million. With royalties.

1 year goes by.

1980: Bette dies.

So sad. But she will go down in history as the inventor of White-Out, as the woman who, essentially, helped to fix history's mishaps.

Though White-Out doesn't really *change* history, it covers it up so we can hide the oversights and redo it all correctly. Close enough. What other choice do we have?

Because while we may be tempted to at times rewrite the past, to give stories to the historyless, the blanks are still there, those historical mistakes aren't going anywhere. Yes, the roots of a language that can harm so many may try to be forgotten, but nothing can be deleted. Just covered.

Palimpsests and carbon copies, however, can be beautiful things. Records of what we have made, making traces of things in the making. Confirmations of yes, this happened. Documenting that this, this right now, *is* happening. How lovely to know there are testaments to the fact that we exist. As I wrote those sentences, though, I used the *Delete* key quite a bit. Finding the right word, replacing "verifications" with "confirmations," "proofs" with "records," and switching "witnessing" to "documenting." But you wouldn't know this if I hadn't written that last sentence.

Computers, while revolutionary, are deceiving. We can't *Ctrl+A+Delete* history. We can't select all of the misogyny and racism that we wish didn't exist and do away with it. Altering the long and strong history of oppressive social constructions isn't that easy. No matter what we try to battle, try to eradicate what's wrong. The historical acts that created these struggles are still there, will always be there, lurking beneath the layer of new language that tries to get us to forget. Because history is etched into our appearance.

Un-alterability.

(Lexicon point)

Wiping out oppression will never be an option as the history of hierarchies will never be forgotten. We can't dismiss the connotations of our skin, the burden our bodies bear.

We can't make a hurricane not happen. We can't un-sexism society.

But we can point out the ways in which mistakes have been sloppily whited out. As in, *the refugees had a place to go.* (But they lost their hope in the Superdome.) As in, *females can be ministers now.* (But misogyny is still preached.) As in, *we have a black president so racism no longer exists.* Wrong. The history of oppression will never leave our collective memories. And yet we can still attempt to right the wrongs, to try to shift language, to eradicate the future need for White-Out.

Here, let me un-mistake that delusion for you.

(Lexicon point)

Point: we can't recreate history, but we can honor the historyless. We can point out what's been missing to bring it back into focus. To revitalize it. We wait for the paint to dry, the pain to heal, and we have hope that this time we'll get it right.

Sally forth.

Susan B. Anthony: Leader. Reformer. Inciter.
    Susan Faludi: Humanist. Journalist. Feminist.
    Susan Sontag: Icon. Activist. Inquisitor.
    All of these Susans changed history.
    None of these Susans were lazy.

I have a dream that at some point certain phrases will become
unwanted. Unused. Archaic.
    Such as:
    A form-fitting white ribbed tank top worn by men.
    The company calls it an *A-Tank*.
    Sometimes, I slip.
    I can't quite quit nomenclature.
    Wife beater.

Well slap my ass and call me Susan.

TRIGGER HAPPY

The back of the book is your **warning**:

Lacy Johnson was held prisoner in a soundproofed room in a basement apartment that her ex-boyfriend rented and outfitted for the sole purpose of raping and killing her. She escaped, but not unscathed. The Other Side *is the haunting account of a first passionate and then abusive relationship, the events leading to Johnson's kidnapping and imprisonment, her dramatic escape, and her hardfought struggle to recover. At once thrilling, terrifying, harrowing, and hopeful,* The Other Side *. . . [provokes] both troubling and timely questions about gender roles and the epidemic of violence against women.*

To: Lacy M. Johnson
From: Chelsey Clammer
May 20, 2014
12:22 p.m.

Hi Lacy,

First, a bit about me: I have my MA in women's studies from Loyola University Chicago, my BA in English and feminist studies from Southwestern University in Georgetown, Texas (a feminist studies degree from a cowtown in Texas? Yes. It exists. Go Texas.), and I am currently enrolled in the Rainier Writing Workshop MFA program. Aside from all of that, I am a feminist (though I'm becoming less certain of that term) who has also been diagnosed with PTSD, an eating disorder and bipolar disorder, and I'm also a fabulously recovering alcoholic.

I tell you all of this so you have a general idea of where I'm coming from. I just finished reading *The Other Side* and I was a) amazed by its unrelenting vulnerability and questioning, b) engaged with its complexities, c) struck by the magnitude of your damn fine prose, and d) suspended reading every fifty pages or so by the necessity to breathe deeply in order to give my body a little self-care respite upon reading this intense material.

While reading *The Other Side*, I also read a *New York Times* article that was posted a few days ago about how UC Santa Barbara and a few other colleges are considering making it a requirement for professors to put trigger warnings in their syllabi. Personally, I am against the idea. This has not always been my position on the matter. Right after a sexual assault, I thought every piece of literature or film needed a trigger warning on it. Now, though, I believe that because it's impossible to put a trigger warning on the entire world, efforts should be concentrated on how one can take care of oneself when reading triggering material. Unfortunately, there is always going to be violence in the world. It will continue to exist if we continue to avoid it. In other words, violence is a fact, so how can we react to it and work with it in a sustainable way? I don't think trigger warnings are the answer.

. . . I'd like to interview you . . .

You know the book is going to be triggering. You know the book is about rape and violence and will be emotionally hard to get through. You know this because you read the book's description. Its synopsis is your warning. You probably shouldn't read this. And yet. You heed these **warnings.** You open the book and encounter words and language and stories and realities that defy the idea that a **warning** can temper the truth. Your only preparation for reading this memoir is your willingness to enter it. (And your use of the second person point of view is your way to get a little bit of distance from it, to protect yourself just a tad from trauma stuff, to not completely dissociate to the point that you don't remember what point you were trying to make in the first place.)

> When [the man who will kidnap and rape me] is home, he wants to fuck: in the morning, at lunchtime, after school, before bed. I say no, or turn away, or if I find some reason to be out of the house all day, we're up until three in the morning, him screaming at me the whole time, twisting my words until they tell a story I've never heard before, until I doubt myself, until I finally give in, and let him fuck me while I sob face-first into my pillow. Our polite Asian neighbors never complain, never look me in the eye. (97)

There are no **warnings**, no cushions that could soften the strength of Johnson's candor.

Though maybe this would work:

Warning: blatancy.

    [After the kidnapping and rape] all I want is someone to fuck me senseless, to pound me until I'm raw and shaking. I want to be held down, pushed aside, flipped over, and smacked. I want to be choked, chained, tied to the floor. I want to bruise, to bleed, to cry out *please stop please don't stop*. I want him to leave after it's done. And then I'll stand up, take a shower, turn on the television. (133)

But how can an author provide a **warning** for something she doesn't even want to name?

    [It's easy to write] how he kidnapped and raped me, how he murdered my cat in our kitchen, how he threatened to abandon me in a foreign country. . . . It's easy to write that I'm afraid of him. . . . It's hard to admit that I loved him. (87–8)

⊢————————————⊣

"Colleges across the country this spring have been wrestling with student requests for what are known as 'trigger warnings.' Explicit alerts that the material they are about to read or see in a classroom might upset them or, as some students assert, cause symptoms of post-traumatic stress disorder in victims of rape or in war veterans."

This *New York Times* article explains how some professors are fuming. "Trigger warnings, they say, suggest a certain fragility of mind that higher learning is meant to challenge, not embrace." The term "trigger warning" is widely used on feminist blogs with the intention of preparing for upcoming content that might be troubling for survivors of violence to read. The warnings are used as signals, as a pause in the text to let the reader gather gulps of breath, take a break, or to walk away. As if warning words can keep you completely safe. Sane.

Advocates of trigger warnings push to have them included in syllabi so violence survivors will be prepared for intense material, will possibly be saved from having a panic attack or flashback. A trigger warning could warn readers that *The Great Gatsby* contains misogynistic violence, that *Mrs. Dalloway* contains a suicide, or that *Things Fall Apart* contains racism and religious persecution.

The belief is that a trigger warning would be there for the protection of the readers, to keep them safe as they read the troubling material, to help them navigate different topics they might have felt uncertain about how to respond to.

That the art we have made from pain will only incite more terror.

That art's interpretation of trauma won't comfort or help to conceptualize differently, but violate.

Therefore, by stating in this sentence that I know of a woman who was brutally raped by her step-father because she was black and he was a white supremacist and then she committed suicide by slashing her wrists after the rape, by not giving you, the reader, any sort of trigger warning for this story I am now responsible for your emotional reactions.

But I don't know you.

What if, instead, I decided to tell the story of the cute puppy my mother bought me for my fifth birthday? But what if instead of being triggered by stories of sexual violence you got panic attacks from thinking about puppies, because you saw a puppy run over by a truck when you were five and it profoundly altered your spiritual beliefs to the point that you now have unmanageable anxiety when thinking about puppies because it makes you doubt there is any purpose to life, because we're all just going to die?

How can I warn the world of every word I am about to say?

And what if thinking about trigger warnings triggers you?

Warning: this sentence contains the word "warning."

—————————————

Who should be responsible for warning you of your uncertainties?

—————————————

Chelsey Clammer: Where do you think the concept of "responsibility" comes into play when thinking about how/if the writer needs to forewarn her readers about challenging and possibly triggering material in her work?

Lacy M. Johnson: This notion of the writer's responsibility to her audience makes me very uncomfortable. If I have a responsibility to my reader, it's to tell her the truth about my experience, and to do so in a meaningful way. In *The Other Side*, for example, I'm writing about a personal history of sexual violence and domestic abuse. It was painful for me to write this book, and I imagine it is painful to read it. That's intentional, because the truth is that the pain of that experience—of living it, writing it, and learning to move past it—is precisely the point. People will likely feel triggered by this book, but I don't think I make any secret of what it's about. I mean, it's right there on the jacket copy.

You might think I need to be warned when a book I am about to read contains scenes of sexual violence. But really, what I need to be warned about is if a character is named Kelly.

Funny story: I was walking down Wayne Street at 11:00 p.m. after singing karaoke at a bar with my friends. As I walked home in my short brown dress, a man ran up from behind me. He ran up behind me and he grabbed me. And when he grabbed me, he reached his hands up my dress and put his hands *in* me. He filled me with his fingers. And then asked, "Hey baby, what's your name?" The brown dress I was wearing was the exact same dress that the woman who I had a huge crush on that summer also had, although hers was kelly green. This crush wasn't at karaoke the night a stranger assaulted me by plugging his fingers into me, because she was fighting with her girlfriend. Six years after that night, six years full of self-harm and alcohol poisoning and therapy and group therapy and psychiatrists and hospital trips to stitch up cuts I made myself and a couple shots at sobriety until it really stuck and then moving to a different neighborhood then moving to a different state then moving to another state then getting married then moving again and then it's five years later and I'm at a job interview and meet my future coworker.

"Hi. I'm Kelly."

Shivers ricochet through me. I've been through enough DBT groups to know how to regulate my breathing when I feel a panic attack coming on. I feel a panic attack coming on. I regulate my breathing, concentrate on Kelly's lips instead of the flashback that is trying to claw its way through my presence. His hands. The short dress. The interview is short and in ten minutes I'm back inside my car, finally able to sob.

It's not hearing the name "Wayne" or seeing a brown dress that terrifies me. It's not thinking about the stranger and his hands in my body or my friends who supported me through the effects of his hands in my body. It's not karaoke. Sometimes I'm doing so well that I can describe the entire assault and only feel a blip of anxiety. But then five years later I meet a woman named Kelly and I completely lose it.

Chelsey Clammer: As a teacher, how do you approach teaching possibly triggering material?

Lacy M. Johnson: I don't think about course material in terms of its potential to trigger or not trigger. If we're watching a film with a difficult scene, I'll let folks know in advance what to expect and I make clear that if they imagine such a scene will make them uncomfortable, they should feel free to excuse themselves at any time. But I also make clear that this doesn't mean they're excused from thinking or writing about the film, or even that scene in particular. If anything, I push harder on them to think critically about their discomfort in relation to the overall aims of the work.

I'm scared shitless about fishtailing in my truck, crashing into a guardrail and then cracking my skull on the windshield and slowly dying before the paramedics can come and save me. I can't seem to let go of this fear. And yet I still drive in the rain. I can't avoid the fact that I live in this world.

I'm not saying a rape survivor should read books or watch films about rape in order to see if she's "healed."

But sometimes those books fall in our laps. Since we can't always avoid triggers, shouldn't we learn what to do with them?

Chelsey Clammer: Have you ever been triggered by any works of literature, and if so what was your response?

Lacy M. Johnson: Absolutely. In fact, I tend to seek out works of literature with frank and honest discussions of traumatic experiences. I realize that might sound a little twisted, but I have found that by understanding the stress responses I have to literature (or film or visual art for that matter) that confronts the other people's experience of trauma, I feel slightly better equipped to understand my own. I feel empathy for that other person, and the intellectual and emotional work of moving with that person through their grief helps me to navigate my own.

Text as mirror. There I am, on the page. There is my experience. The details are different, and the words are ones I wouldn't have thought to use, but there I am. Reflected. Held. Connected.

There's more about how we find strength in other people who will not allow themselves to be silenced. About how we can get through those moments full of fright by knowing that other people have survived. That they have put words to what I have not yet figured out how to describe.

This is about more than sharing an experience with the world. This is about more than a reader feeling like someone gave her experience a voice. This is about understanding how we can't actually control anything. The world happens. And we're happening in this world. We need to learn how to work with these things.

Push harder to think critically about your discomfort.

Chelsey Clammer: Writing is a way to heal from trauma, but what about reading?

Lacy M. Johnson: I don't think I could have written *The Other Side* (nor would I have felt compelled to) without the brave work of women whose work found me when I most needed it—Alice Sebold, Kathryn Harrison, Lidia Yuknavitch, Sarah Manguso, Mary Karr. I've never met these women, and yet their words—difficult and painful as they were—came as a great comfort to me in a time of terrible doubt and fear.

I surround myself with books that are hard to open, but even harder to put down once I've journeyed through them.

A STRIKING RESEMBLANCE

But I was talking about lightning. There. Between us. Magnetic flux. The density of our different desires tethering us together. I am pulled towards him. My compass, oriented. We lie in his field of attraction. I travel and re-travel to him, again. And again.

There's the metaphor of the magnet. The fact of how each has its magnetic moment. The pull, the touch. The continual drawing closer. Lured into that field—the magnetic one in which I enter, then his urge to me, (though not yet) (the tenacious wait), then we meet, then the two of us tumble together towards the fact of connection, the fact of attraction. His decision. He comes to me. Fact. Magnets interact.

Also, there's the spark.

What a cliché.

I will use it anyway.

The spark, its force, the need. Magnetic moment. Tactility.

Suppose I were to tell you he only touched me once.

Suppose I were to tell you I haven't seen him since.

Suppose I were to tell you his hands have yet to recede.

Magnetic. Two energies charging, building, colliding. Then striking. It's how electricity is conceived.

A tremendous electrical buildup in clouds is what concocts lightning. The electricity stews, brews. And then it is ready. Lightning channels escort it to the ground. The taxiing of manic energy. The surge of lightning leaves evidence of its existence behind, everything touched now magnetized. Its unique magnetic signature stamps itself on the world; then the lightning quickly retreats like part of a pair in a one-night stand, leaving in the air behind it that charged magnetic feeling that something happened here. Perhaps at times we can still feel it. That flash of an influence. There is no going back.

About the lightning.

About how there was that magnetic charge, *once*. About how he almost came back.

About how he does now, differently. A different kind of flash.

After our magnets (somehow) pulled away from each other, the grasp released, the weeks spent alone, and then more weeks spent alone, holed up in my apartment, grieving. When I re-enter the world, I look for him everywhere. Strangers shapeshift for a second. *Him. That's him.* Maybe. No. I become curious about my attraction to him, how it is I have come to consider the creation of that magnetic moment as something called *we*. How it is that I continue to feel the crackling buzz of his touch imprinted in my skin. My veins ache. How did this happen? It was twofold. (And I think of me, folding beneath him. Somatic submission.) First, a microscopic effect. Ampere model. As in, atomic, circular currents, the effects of his touch that still swirl inside me, regardless. Then, the macroscopic. A curl of electrical current flowing around the surface. As in, our skin. The lure. His no resistance. His travels to *there*.

I dive further into the definition, wanting to know the specifics of this specific attraction—him, his hands, his only chance—to understand it, yes, to make it a part of me, yes, to make sense of how I continue on with the pronoun *we*, regardless. Even in his absence. *We*. I search. And what I find is language unfurling along my tongue. Ineluctable. Ebullient. The poetry of potency. The intensity that reeled him in. Hands fishing for flesh.

Yes, the flux of my compass.

Yes, his touch, how it will never leave me.

Orientation swayed.

White veins crackle across the sky.

The artistry of lightning striking the skin. How it races through the path of least resistance. Even in human bodies. Especially in human bodies. The taxiing quality of veins. Lightning enters, then follows the trajectory of blood. The bolt's graffiti marks its course through the maze of veins, leaving a small replica of itself. The evidence of tissue damage proves its accomplishment. The impression it made on human flesh.

A tattoo you deserved (you were struck by lightning, after all), but didn't really want (who wants to be struck by lightning?).

How does this happen?

Georg Christoph Lichtenberg.

He was a man with a malformation of the spine. A hunchback. Unusually short. And the malformation grew worse, his affected breath shallowed in his chest.

But before his lungs exhaled that final short breath, in 1777 this German man named Lichtenberg conducted experiments to discover how struck skin showcases electrical strokes. He built an electrophorus—a device consisting of two plates. An electrical charge was rubbed into the dielectric plate. A second metal plate was placed on that charge. Electricity occurred. Lichtenberg constructed the biggest electrophorus that would ever be built. He needed the space to implement his experiments, a site large enough to capture the magnitude of his discoveries: six feet in diameter. Within this giant electrophorus, he produced sparks to find an explanation for how lightning leaves its mark on human flesh. He named his answer xerography.

There were insular surfaces involved. As in, resin, glass, rubber. A powdered sulfur was placed on the surface. Since sulfur is slightly negative, it has an attraction to those positive insular surfaces. Friction occurs. A polarity is seen. What this means: the electrical charges stuck to the surface, and the site of electricity could finally be seen. And the sights were star-like. Lightning-like.

The skin is an insular surface. It catches the negative force of lightning. An attraction occurs. A touch. And in that moment the skin is scarred. Lightning engraves.

Veins like creeks branching off a river. Tree branches, perhaps. But really, tributaries. A resemblance to lightning in the sky. When lightning strikes skin, when nature's assault on the body has retreated, when it walks away from its one chance, when the lightning survivor wakes up in a hospital and looks down at her body, what she sees is the tattoo of lightning's trajectory. How it has revealed her circulatory system. The mark of tissue damage looking like creeks swerving from rivers. Like tree branches, sprouting. Tributaries. Veins like lightning crackling across the sky.

———

Because I want to talk about lightning.

I want to talk about that magnetic moment.

I want to talk about him.

I want to talk about how he imprinted himself on my skin, how my veins still rattle with him.

How touch is shocking, fast and effective.

An electric touch translated in my body in the space of two-tenths of a second. The time it takes to realize a touch. Two-tenths of a second leading to a surge of a connection that lasts. This is about him, his touch, his one chance. The flash.

This is how it happens. His touch interrupts the way my body is walking. The feel of the summer night breeze swishing the hem of my cotton dress, kissing my thighs, is forgotten in the moment of his one chance. A touch. An alteration, a new reorientation. First, he compasses me. Here is my body adjusting to the significance of his feet running up behind me (and his quadriceps flex, his hamstrings elongate, determined feet propel him forward, towards me, his body full of movement, of want, of an undeniable, unstoppable magnetic pull). He pushes the feel of the summer night breeze out of my mind. Out of sight. His sight. His clear sight. There. He strikes. How did he know this was his one chance? How long did he watch me walking, his plan brewing? Stewing. An irresistible lure. His feet then running. What turned him on? What jolted him in my direction? In a brief moment my muscles clench, my neck a nexus of startle that quickly spreads. My nerves showing the way. The reflex occurs.

Two-tenths of a second.

The violence of his storm.

The magnetic pull of him towards me. His hands on me. Tactility.

He delivers his whisper, "Hey baby what's your name?" The rumble in me outpours. A roar. The hands still hold on. The whisperer inquires again. I scream.

Thunder is caused by lightning.

There is a sequence here. The alignment of lightning with thunder, then with the rain that follows. But sometimes syzygy doesn't occur. Sometimes thunder holds in, swallows its sobs.

Consider the concept of safety. When should I seek shelter after hearing thunder? Use the "Flash-to-Bang" method, they say. The number of seconds between the striking light and the rumble of thunder. One Mississippi. Two Mississippi. Each second, a mile. The feel of the air shifts—as when an electrical storm prepares to pursue. How long until I should seek safety? Thirty seconds, they say.

(Two-tenths of a second.)

The rumble of thunder.

I like that.

Sounds like poetry.

But I was rumbling on about lightning.

(Dissociation momentarily done.)

(Crawling out from behind the safety blanket of facts and poetics of weather.)

The violence of his storm. The roar of my *please no* moan. Then, my energy gathered for my *leave now* crackle.

The spark, a cliché.

I have to use it anyway.

The spark, its force, the need. Magnetic moment. Tactility.

Suppose I told you he only touched me once.

Suppose I told you I haven't seen him since.

Suppose I told you his hands have yet to recede.

Suppose I told you my hackles are still heightening.

Better to be safe than sorry.

What could have been the startling stimuli (all of that flexing, elongating, determined feet propelling him forward, towards me, the lure, all heard in his footsteps) did not actually startle me. I should have turned around when I heard footsteps pounding. What finally made me react? A grabbing hand. A shaken shoulder. A body electrocuted by shock. Tissue damage.

Here, my body responds without my say.

I become a surge of sensory synapses. Inside, cells circulate around the feel of him on me.

Him on me.

Fingers like magnets.

He draws me nearer.

There. On the tip of my shoulder. His fingers find their place in this world.

And then his voice.

His voice like a lover's heavy breath blanketing my skin. Soft, almost. He whispers his request. "Hey baby, what's your name?" Perhaps for a moment it was like heat lightning, a caressing strike spreading silently across the sky.

And there is the fact of his other hand.

As where the hem of my dress shames itself. It is not long enough.

His hand as it finds its way. One set of fingers caressing my shoulder, one set reaching up, underneath, from behind me. The short dress.

Think: bowling ball.

He reaches in, tries to break the barrier of brown cotton dress. Thumb there. Finger here. Into the holes he tries to dig. His hands reaching, searching, curious as to how much distance within me he can achieve. The stimuli.

Magnetic. Two energies charging, building, colliding. Then striking. It's how electricity is conceived.

I thunder.

After his hands retreat, my life becomes a series of aftershocks. Residual storms. Panic attacks. I turn to poetry.

Why? Because poetry is a different language. Poetry provides a reprieve from his image. The ability to see the beauty of a line, to stop between the stanzas, and breathe. Or hide.

Anne Carson:
I stand amid glaciers.
Listen to the wind outside
falling towards me from the outer edges and space.
I have no theory
of why we are here.

Adrienne Rich:
what does it mean "to survive"
A cable of blue fire ropes our bodies
burning together in the snow We will not live
to settle for less We have dreamed of this
all of our lives

Jorie Graham:
it is here, only here,

      in this gap

between us,
that the body of who we are
to have been

      emerges: imagine:

she lets him go

Why am I here?
    To survive? To let him go?
    To not settle for less?
    I'm learning the poetics of pain.

And how lightning can, in fact, strike the same spot twice.

Long after he is gone, long after he walks away and turns the corner, after three years of therapy, he still strikes me. Again. And again. And again. One Mississippi. The storm returns each night. Two Mississippi. I waited too long, found no shelter, no place to seek safety. Three Mississippi.

After he grabbed me, after I did not tell him my name, after I thundered, after I turned around to face him, my shoulder then released, his fingers jerking out of me, I looked into the shadows of his eyes.

Lured into that field—the magnetic one in which I entered, then his urge to me (though not yet) (the tenacious wait), then we met, then the two of us tumbled together towards the fact of connection, the fact of his attraction. His decision. He came to me. Fact. Magnets interact.

My compass, oriented. I travel and re-travel to him. The flashbacks. Magnetic.

In two-tenths of a second he hardened me. I stand still now, on guard, stand expectant, watching him fade away—momentarily. He turned the corner. I will never see him again. I will see him every day. My body no longer moves fluidly, freely. It feels like glass. Solid but with the potential to shatter. I am waiting for the next *him*, the possibility of another spark.

The spark.

What a cliché.

I have no choice but to use it, anyway.

The spark, its force, his need. Magnetic moment. Tactility. His eyes.

I am hardened.

Alchemized.

Fulgurites.

Sand melts. 3,002 degrees. That would be Fahrenheit. On a conductive surface, the lightning fuses grains of sandy earth together. These fuses accumulate to create another element. Sand to glass. Alchemy.

One could say *lightning* is *petrifying*.

Inhale.

Prepare.

Now, petrified.

├────────────────┤

But there's more to talk about, more about this lightning.

How something sparked between us. A magnifying event. Him drawn to me. Me unable to get away from the memory of his magnetic moment. Years later I will have gone through many lovers. Many hands will have touched my clothes, helped to tear this dress from my flesh, in just a flash.

But it will be his hands I remember best. *Our* flash of a moment lingers. Yes, his fingers.

His attention to me so profound that in a different context it might be considered devotion. His grabbing attention gratified me, no matter how much I didn't want it. Living in a body I never considered attractive, enticing, I couldn't dismiss this feeling of being chosen. My body—the focal point of his attention. He chose me to be the one to feel his touch. Magnetic. My response—enlightening.

I want to talk about a different man now.

Roy Cleveland Sullivan died five months, six days, and a handful of hours after I was born. He was from a place I have never heard of, Shenandoah National Park. Virginia. That's where he chose to stay, to live, to work. A park ranger.

A lightning survivor.

And not just a one-time survivor of that rare occurrence, but on *seven* different occasions the lightning stroked him, jolted him. He survived each time.

And then he died. How? Did the *seven* doses of lightning's assault finally overpower him? This man, this "Human

Lightning Conductor," this man named Roy who became a human lightning rod, who found his place in world record books because of the *seven* times, was not killed by lightning. What killed him was the self-directed gunshot wound to the head at the age of seventy-one. Perhaps it was about an unrequited love. Lack of love. If only he could have seen what did love him, the huge bouts of lightning that just couldn't stay away. His body and brain fried from the seven times. Add to that a lover who perhaps wanted nothing to do with his tissue-damaged skin, did not want to look at the sight of his veins tattooed onto him like lightning crackling across the sky. Scarred lightning. Maybe at seventy-one he got a case of the fuckits. A flash of a plan. A bang of its execution.

———

I have to tell you more about the thunder and lightning, after. Its proximity. One mile per second. I count to seven Mississippi, then hear the rumbles coming.

It is two weeks after his touch, then it is two months, then two years.

Right now, three years after, a violent storm charging down from the sky.

I stare at it through my window, stare at the storm. I want more striking. A boom to bludgeon the thought of him.

I want to be the one this time, the one who has the say, the one who controls the touch.

I want that magic, that power. To redirect the storm.

In my bedroom, I raise my index finger to the glass, not quite touching its pane. My hand hovers. Then, I move my finger in a jagged line, Z it a couple of times. Z's like zaps of lightning.

Z.

Shockingly, lightning strikes in the trajectory of my fingered Z. There, on that one blade of grass my Z had been pointing at, the energy enters the ground.

Magic.

Instant light. Instant sound.

No countable seconds.

A quick occurrence.

Nothing can be done about it.

About him.

Twenty-five million strokes of lightning are created during some 100,000 annual storms.

A hundred bolts in every second.

And how this energy affects humans.

The odds are 1 in 960,000.

Roy was seventy-one.

Odds in your lifetime of being struck by the crackling white light are 1 in 13,000.

Something thought Roy was special. How it always found him. How it singled him out.

Between the dates of his life, 1959–2003, there were 3,696 lightning-related deaths.

Roy should be on that list. But he survived. And he waited until after he survived to die.

Ten percent of lightning victims are killed.

Seventy percent suffer serious long-term effects.

Like Roy, perhaps. Like his death, perhaps. An unrequited love.

And what about me? How I was struck. What are the odds of sexual assault?

One in four.

This strikes me.

—————————————

Later, after weeks and months and then three years, my skin still cannot stop counting the two-tenths of a second.

The meaning of the ruminating obtains a diagnosis.

DSM IV does the defining.

I have a number now.

309.81.

PTSD.

—————————————

I am talking about lightning.

A phenomenon, yet common. Spectacular, but deadly. A reaching out. This is not completely understood. Three million flashes of lightning occur each day around the world. Three million right conditions. (He sees her. She does not see him. One in four women.)

Veins crackle across the sky.

The idea of *we* builds up. I cannot strike it out of me. PTSD.

The brain continues making the connections, again. And again. And again. And then three years later and then still, the synapses.

And then still, the synapses.

And again.

The synapses.

Snap out of it.

This is about lightning.

There. Between us. Magnetic flux. The density of our different desires tethering us together. I am pulled towards him. My memories compassed.

Look at this.

This.

This is about lightning.

No.

This.

This is about a reprieve.

About not settling for less. About knowing why I am here.

To no longer hide.

To let him go.

Now, recede.

To find the calm after his _____.

I COULD TITLE THIS WAVERING

I don't know if you'll like this.

Sidestepping the use of *affect* and *effect*, I evade discomposure that would surely come from showcasing what I don't know but should. Regardless of my higher education in English, as well as my even higher education in creative writing, I still cannot remember when to use *affect* or *effect*. Sure, I can name sound effects. And I know a face and demeanor create a person's affect. But there are other nefarious ways in which to use these terms. Actually, I'm not quite sure if *nefarious* is the word I want. I'm not quite sure if I know *nefarious*'s meaning. I'll go look it up. I just looked it up. *Nefarious* has nothing to do with this. Though I liked the way it sounded in that sentence.

Once, I heard a writer say I should put my ear to the page. Actually, he (she? I don't remember who the writer was) was not talking to me specifically, but to a room full of writers in which I was sitting. I would like to think we were all listening, collectively learning something about how sound and reverberations saturate our mouth, cascade out.

Effect to me is more pleasurable to pronounce than *affect*. *Affect* reminds me of those commercials with a talking duck pressuring me to get insurance. I am unsure if the advertisement is affective (?), though perhaps it is because I think about that duck each time I am hesitant of which word to use. I am often hesitant of which word to use. I am wound up by this. It creates a wound in my writer-capability confidence. Choosing the right word, at the right time—all of this is something of which I will always be unsure.

And so I avoid all use of effect and affect. Instead, I use words relatively similar in meaning. I wonder how this ~~affects~~ ~~effects~~ impacts my writing, my writing's meanings.

Either way, I'm in command of this essay's language, even if it is to cover up my lingual uncertainties. Still, it's my say. I dictate how to hide my grammatical failures.

I don't know if you'll like this.

The effect (?) of this, of my absent confidence, coils in me. Tight. Tangled with truth and myth—rules and conventions—too knotted to separate the decrees from how I write. My pages present as comprehensible, perhaps even intriguing, but underneath those polished, published sentences is shame for not knowing the laws of language and elements of style— for all of those sins of syntax I commit on every page. Always. You read slick words that satisfy your need for rich writing, but underneath it all is a hollow self-confidence. Or its opposite. This is where the anxiety nests. Fear of being found out, of how this costume of polished composition, these slick words that lay atop a lack of self-confidence, will one day be apparent. Liar identity revealed. The foundation from which my writing struggles to grow is embedded with these uncertainties that bully me. Yes, I am wound too tight by worries and second-guessings. Yes, I know this is a wound of mine. The smooth statements others make about my writing should soothe me. If I were to hear them. But what I hear is a chink opening, silently. It reveals a previously undisclosed part of me. The same part that insists praise is really rejection. And rejection screams itself into my presence. Always. A fact. A loudly vetoing voice. Judgment screeching, jarring.

I want an unsounding.

Unwind.

Uncoil.

I'm not sure how to do this.

I waver.

I'm not going to get all lugubrious over this, though it appears that I'm tending to get all loquacious over this, because apparently words are what I hide behind, and create how I consider the world.

For instance:

Every time I write *wind* I get confused by which meaning I mean to make. A river can wind. As in around. I would like to think a river can wind, as in push, gust, a gesture of intentions that lunges onward, towards me—its character encouraging. The river does this for me. It winds forth a rallying draft of air—strong, though subtle. I can't see it, but I can feel how it moves me, wants to be a part of me, flows through me. This is about spirituality. Or perhaps learning. How a body grows so slowly until it stops growing, but how inside that body a mind is maturing quickly. Rapidly. Repeatedly.

Stagnancy giving space for progress. I find these things profound. What calm incites. What silence screams. How even when water is at a standstill, I still sense the breeze that offers me its deeds. Its whisper. The river still, as in sound subdued. The din dimmed. Hushed. Though it speaks to me. The river winds through me, winds around me. Still.

And about that previous sentence, that *still*. Is that the meaning I meant to make?

Maybe.

I don't know.

You should know this is the only time I'll mention *homonym*. You should know I do not know how to pronounce that.

What I do know, though, is that at some point I will need to stop thinking about my unripe vocabulary, green grass of conventions—and my youthful (?) suspicions of them. To just write. Let me reiterate how I know I get wound up too tightly by these nebulous meanings. Yes, I know this.

Yet again, I don't know if I'm using the right word. (Right now, it would be easy to discuss the right ways to write. The rites of writing and that moment when you know writing is what's right for you, and so that's what you do.) Does *nebulous* encompass what I am trying to get at? Perhaps I should study the *n* section of the dictionary which includes *nab* and *nymphomania* and everything in between those bookends of words beginning with *n*, brought to you by the dictionary. Either way, I'm thinking of clouds. I don't know if that's what you're thinking of.

I don't know if you'll like this, either.

No one ever told me the laws of verbs. No one ever told me you can't verb a noun, that you can't Chelsey a sentence. And I would like to think you can noun anything, as well. The power to name the important actions we point to for meaning. To creep around the myths of composition. I live on a whisper.

I was going to say something about *despite*. How despite the *e*, *respite* is pronounced differently. The caboosed vowel silenced, censored, the reasons for which I do not know, the ones that incite my incorrectness. Then, someone notices. Then, the *minute* number of *minutes* in which I once, maybe, perhaps, felt assured of my pronunciation, that yarn of writer confidence *wound* around my vocabulary's *broche*, until I am corrected. Then, my voice feels vulnerable, exposed. Raw. As if so many years of mispronunciation has grated through it, leaving a *wound* so harsh no *troche* could soothe it. I stand corrected by my companion's quizzical look, those raised eyebrows that say, *You're a writer. How could you not know how to pronounce that?* As if I can hear a word by sight. Still, regardless, chastisement. I *cache* the *ache* of writer embarrassment deep within me. Hide it. But how am I to know when an ending *e* is on hiatus?

Silence.

The absence of any noise. Stillness. Muteness. Omission. Oblivion.

The state of being forgotten.

Secret.

That which is concealed. Clandestine. Undisclosed. Masked.

Those *kuh*-sounding delineations of silence pronounced, of making silence so pronounced.

The definition of silence is loud.

?

One should mention *irony*.

As in, *abbreviation*. By which I mean *abbreviation* = *abbr.* Twelve letters strung together that define how we don't have time for all of this—this stringing of twelve letters together to produce a term. Plus everything else that surrounds it. Permeates it. Elongates it. Such as life. How at times there is too much life to handle and so we take a break. brb. And then we return to the page, to life, to ourselves and figure out a way to keep going, to keep up. To make things easier for ourselves. e.g. i.e. a.m. p.m. Mrs. &. etc.

There is no time for *abbreviation*.

There was another point to be made, aside from all of this. Despite all of this. I do not remember what.

Still.

I would like to think a river can pause its flow. A brief rest before it goes. Re: growth.

Still, these are the things I don't know.

I know I'm really into verbs and nouns right now. Which is to say writing. Pen to page then fingers to keys, QWERTY-ing. Right now, I am uncertain of my verb and noun usage in the same way I am uncertain if my body could stay standing when standing in line at the post office. Can I ever do things correctly? Even faintly? My uncertainty about my line-formation abilities unnerves me. I waver. Here is the story: the last time I stood in line at the post office I wavered, then fainted. Right now, I am in the predicament of not knowing if I can stand going to the post office again, to stand while I'm in line, again. Some part of me believes I'm now destined to faint each time I step into that building with its muted patriotic color scheme—the faint red, gray, the dull blue. Now, I raise my mug of coffee to my lips and sip, considering, spilling just a bit. I correct myself, place my lips on the rim just right, ready for the downward slide of liquid. Like when my body went downward, waterfall-like, I suppose. Though I am uncertain of this—at that point I had yet to un-faint.

What I remember from my last visit to the post office is relief and a smile in my dreams. How my shaking, wavering body snapped into a type of sleeping, one that felt so good. I don't know how long I slept. They said I hit my head on the counter on my way down. This was after I dropped my packages and after the woman in line behind me wondered why I had dropped my packages until my body crashed to the tiles and then she understood. The winding line of Christmas packages waiting to move on to their next location found this fall more than faintly troublesome. 9-1-1 was called. I woke up to a crowd of concerned faces. I woke up to an excuse tumbling out of my lips. "I'm famished." Who says that?[9]

That is not a lie. It's a story. One of mine. As a reader I suppose you can't be certain about the difference between what this story is and what it might not be. All I can claim is that this writing is this—whatever *this* is. Fact or fiction, it still exists.

Once, sometime a few weeks ago, I was disappointed in my skin as I rode up the middle section of a three-tiered

---

9. Someone who uses fancy words to distract people from asking *why*, from investigating the precursors.

escalator. The decorative holes in my jeans (a style titled *distressed*) stretched tighter than what I thought was appropriate. Though allowing my flesh to expand keeps me from fainting again.

Once, a few sentences ago, I was disappointed by the two dots of coffee that dropped on my white shirt when I raised mug to lips and sipped, considering, spilling just a bit.

Once, two paragraphs ago, I was uncertain about how to spell *disappointed* (Two *s*'s or two *p*'s? Please don't ask me how to spell *Massachusetts*. I cannot do this without spell check's assistance.) And I also used the wrong road/rode and whole/hole a few paragraphs ago.[10] For some reason, I don't find this disappointing even though I have thirty-one years of experience of getting to know words. Re: growth. And how I might not be able to remember a name, but it's nice to meet you anyway, again.

I don't know if you'll like this.

I'm still debating if I can stand going to the post office this morning. I have put the mug down and stuck a cigarette to my lips as I consider what to do in this moment.

In this moment, I have an Eminem song stuck in my head. I probably shouldn't have revealed that. I like to let readers believe the soundtrack to my writing is soundless, that my words can sing on their own. The symphony of my sentences. I am the conductor. Though perhaps this isn't the case. My rap habit now revealed. Please, don't judge me.

I have more to say about wound and wound. (I thought of this sentence when I was blowing my nose on my finger

---

10. Fixed it!

just now but trying not to because that's gross. But I didn't feel as if I could walk over to my bathroom to get a Kleenex. For one thing, I don't have Kleenex in my bathroom. In this household I use toilet paper to blow my nose. For another, I'm still smoking a cigarette, its red tip smoldering towards my lips, and it seemed like it would be bad form to bring my toxic cigarette into the bleached, sterile bathroom, even though each day I sit at my desk and blow the smoke in that direction, always. So I slightly blew my nose on my finger. I want to emphasize *slightly*. I don't know if that word makes a difference in your perception of me. Most certainly, though, if I had said *always* instead of *slightly* you would have stopped reading, not wanting to hear any more of this—this disgusting image so distracting. Thus, *slightly*.)

Personally, I find that parenthetical funny.

I don't know if you'll like this. Still.

I don't know if I'll still like this when I enter the editing phase. I wonder how this wavering impacts my writing. I wander around the wavering, observe its meaning. How necessary it is to know the difference between an *o* and an *a*. English is the hardest language to learn. I don't know if this is true, but it's what I'm told (in English). What I know is that selecting then stitching vocabulary in such a way as to make all of this weaving seem simple is actually quite a complicated task. A life of jacquard language created without a Jacquard loom. The quilted essays may look complete, but look closely at that stitching. It wasn't done by a steady hand. I am starting to realize this. I feel as if I should write the word *swath* somewhere in here. Though it's not necessary. And the sound of it doesn't even fit. Irresolution looms.

Ear to page.

Update: I just put out my cigarette, though I no longer need to blow my nose. I wonder if you were hoping I would never again mention this facet of my slightly snotty finger flesh. Sorry to disappoint you.

I have more to say about *wound* and *wound*. Mostly because I just noticed I say "wound" first, and then "wound" second. Always. Because you're reading this, because you're not hearing me speak this, you probably can't figure out my word order preference. Keep your ear to the page. Come closer. You can find me under the whisper.

I don't know if you'll like this unveiling.

Unraveling.

Undoing.

I know I am wound too tight. I know this is a wound of mine. This unsure part of me. How the nerves screw up, tie up in me, cinch around me as I think about vocabulary. And grammar. And syntax. And semicolons. And sentence structure. And point of view and passive voice and punctuation and past tense. These things make me tense. After each attempt to be linguistically correct, I come away more confused. I don't know what to do about this. I know I don't like this.

Fuck it.

Now, an ending's push:

I don't know if you like elucidated uncertainties. Such as this.

Such as a confession of such ignorance, fessing up to not knowing the rules and standards. How unwriterly of me. One last confession: I stand here, at the end of it all, a bit unnerved by this revealing—(still?) wavering.

One last admission: I ~~defy~~ sneak around linguistic myths with such softness, so subtly, there is no ~~resistance~~ notice. That is where my writing ~~strikes~~ is.

Still.

CIRCADIAN

Worn tracks in the carpet that cannot be vacuumed away. The path of pacing. A trail that traces the proof of pain's presence. Persistence.

Think strapped down, chained up, locked away—think powerless. Enslaved by the need to pace. Trapped in a cycle, walking circles around the pain at 2:00 a.m., trying to assuage a headache, one that insomnia only intensifies, yet sleep is impossible with such throbbing, clobbering. Pace around and grasp the fact that suicide is the only cure, but not yet, not when there is still a sliver of hope that something will work, that even though it's palliative, pacing will eventually alleviate. One hopes.

Keep pacing.

Because pain exacerbates when stagnant. Just *sitting with it* is not an option. If all motion stops, the ache then congregates, an angry mob pounding at every crevice in the skull. Thanatotic thump. So keep pacing. Proceed on that trampled path. The crushed carpet—a symptom of cluster headaches.

Then, an abrupt pause as knees crash onto carpet, fists pound floor, head bangs ground, the carpet too matted down to be a soft place where a head can land.

After an hour and a half of pacing, the ferocious palpitations evaporate. Momentarily. But they return, again, always, always again, but first those eight minutes of relief. Exactly eight. Clockwork. No one knows why cluster headaches take eight-minute breaks, but they do and it's true for most who are afflicted with this incurable illness. Eight minutes and too soon the recess is ruined by the next cluster coming. One minute left. Inhaling, exhaling, praying to a god that possibly doesn't even exist. Inhale. Exhale. Here it comes.

Clockwork.

Then clusters raid, persist, recreate a chaos that won't unclench, unclamp, unclasp. So tenacious. Squeezed tight, squeezed right there—right behind the right eye. Nothing can be done.

The hows and whys of cluster headaches are unknown.

Pain with a mind of its own.

———————————————

I was there.

A moment occurs that will change my life, but not at first, not right then. Instead, there will be the moment and there will be the ten years in which the results of that moment lie dormant. But during that decade, meaning will gather, snowball.

But first, that moment.

I witness the second when my father's head hits metal, hear the ensuing violent gasps. I see skin cut open and watch blood waterfall down his face. Later, I will see his stitches. Much later, the moment's full effect will spring forth.

Ten years after his head injury, a cluster of nerves starts clutching my father. They grip his neck, jaw, face, eyes, temples. He is defenseless. His world slips. Falls. The clusters are soon followed by pacing and alcohol, by oxygen and medication, by anything that might help. Nothing helps. The effect of a head injury squeezes. Yanks. Then the father-shaped space in my life is left blank.

———————

Our relationship becomes a cycle of blame we don't know how to stop.

The cycle of blame:

Ice cream instigates an argument. An argument is our last interaction. Our last interaction is when I'm twenty-one and Dad asks if I want ice cream. Ice cream is something I don't eat. I don't eat ice cream because I'm vegan. Being vegan becomes a symbol of our non-relationship. Our non-relationship consists of one thing: him blaming me for shutting him out and me blaming him for not reaching out. We don't reach out, making our interactions nothing but the same circular argument. The same circular argument. Circular. Argument. Circle. Argue. All of this will only end when he's dead.

He's dead.

But first:

"If you fucking cared to know anything about your daughter, you'd know I don't eat ice cream!" In this last interaction—I'm twenty-one and he's two days into being fifty-four—I resort to acting like a kid, a tantrum bursting. A foot stomping, smashing down carpet to pound anger out of me. I could take this further. I could crash onto the floor and start pounding fists on the ground. Bang my head where there isn't any soft place for it to land. Why? To make a point. To express a pain. How his absentee parenting irks me, invisible-izes me. Him not really caring to see a young woman with whom he shares half his genes. So yeah, I'm angry about the question of ice cream. Disturbed by the fact that my own father hasn't noticed how in the past three years his daughter doesn't drink milk or eat cheese. Plus, no eggs. No sour cream. There's soy in her coffee. Does Dad even know what *vegan* means?

But the metaphor works two ways. I'm not the only kid in this scene. He, the child asking a question about ice cream and me, the adult denying him something sweet.

Nothing sweet ever evolved between us.

After I scream to him about my veganism, after I slam my door to shut him up, shut him out, he pounds his heavy, flat feet down the hall. My mother's name now being called. Echoes of rage hurricane our house.

In the kitchen, she yells: "Jeff, she just doesn't want any ice cream."

In the kitchen, he yells: (words I can't make out—coherence muffled with rage).

In the kitchen, they both yell: (garbled sentences crash into one another, and vehemence circling the one thing I can clearly hear: my name. Such clamor).

And so I scream. And so he screams. And soon we are all screaming about the ice cream.

And a week later he's dead.

Blood-alcohol level = 0.46.

Here come the hypotheticals. The what if I had said *yes*? Because the *no* wasn't a *no* to the sweet dessert, but to him. To the father who knew nothing about his daughter. He knew this. What if this hadn't been true? What if we had worked on having a connection? Could a *yes* have kept him alive?

A few days after he dies, I'm desperate to take back my *no* and turn it into a *yes*. 2:00 a.m. Drunk. I go to the kitchen to say my *yes*, to fill the emptiness I feel from my father's final absence. Standing in front of the freezer, blood swirling with vodka and grief, I grab the cold tub of ice cream, then a spoon, then start to fill. I fill. I freeze and I fill and fill and fill until it's all gone. But there is no *yes* at the bottom of the tub. Only more emptiness, regardless of how full I am. And how later, the next morning, I'll remember this binge and despise myself for putting too much into my body, when all I want is a physical reflection of what's going on inside of me—that emptiness. The father-shaped hollow. I set the spoon in the sink and that's when it comes, charges into me, crashes then cuts through my skull. A searing headache, my forehead now pounding. Cracking. Pain reflecting what I feel inside. The unbearable ache of empty.

An ice cream headache.

Brain freeze.

Nine years old. I stand under the wood deck with Dad—his tall body curving away from the wood's lonely gray shade, my own body fully vertical, head coming up to his hips—and help him stack firewood. This is before helping Dad becomes disheartening. Destructive, even. This is when I don't mind how "helping" means "watching." When I'm not bothered by the silence between father and daughter, when it doesn't feel futile that our conversations are constricted by directives. Hold this screw. Hand me that tool. Here, in this autumn afternoon under the deck, Dad and I are still figuring out the specifics and logistics of our relationship. How a positive bond still feels feasible.

Dad's 6'2" frame arches down, bending at the hips. Dipping hips angle forward his skeleton, those tendons, the soft muscle tissue of this father-shaped mass, all stooping. Above us, the sun stretches across the top of the deck. But here, below its gray underbelly, shadows collect. Not dark, but muted. Muffled. Light holds its breath.

The rest of this scene will unfurl into a space of meaning. It's a moment, a memory that I will mold into an answer for *why* and *when* and *how come*. For what went wrong.

But first, the firewood.

We're stacking it, Jenga-like. Down here, lingering above us is a metal jut of a right angle that, in a moment, his forehead will find.

Here I am, about to see why the future will hold what it holds, how the domino effect jolted into motion the day Dad and I were hunched under the deck. The day when I wasn't necessarily bored, but didn't know why I was there. To observe? To learn? To see my father in motion?

To stand witness to this moment.

It begins.

He un-hunches. His back fully, fatefully unbends, his skull ascends, unaware of what is up, above, the right angle that does him wrong. There is a bang and then a fissure in his forehead flesh. A gash. Skin separated. The future now unknowingly shadowed.

I see dark red blood slowly start to weep out of my father's forehead. In a decade I will see the effects of this: cluster headaches that will incite a suicide. (That blood-alcohol level that was just too high.)

A head injury can cause cluster headaches.

Right now, the open wound is right in front of me. It looks me in the eye.

A silent warning.

Brain freeze.

It's an excruciating zap. A short-lived headache. It occurs when cold substances are ingested quickly. The instant agony only lasts for about ten to twenty seconds, but those moments of pain are painful enough to give this headache its own name. These episodes result from sinus capillaries rapidly cooling and then rewarming, a rebound dilation that sends stinging signals along the trigeminal nerve, through pain receptors in the neck and head straight to the brain. The three-pronged nerve that pulsates on each side of the face, all through the neck, around the lower jaw and behind the eye. Can you see it? It's right there. Agony now embodied.

These headaches are also called "ice cream headaches," as they often occur when ingesting ice cream.

The ice cream company Ben & Jerry's had to rename its "Clusterfluff" flavor to "What a Cluster" since some consumers were offended by the name's close resemblance to "clusterfuck."

"Clusterfuck" is a military term for when things go extremely wrong.

"Clusterheads" are people who suffer from cluster headaches—a type of pain that proves how inside the brain something, anything can go extremely wrong. Cluster headaches (not to compare, not to create a hierarchy of pain—though I will, and I do, because it's necessary, because its severity can kill) have been declared by Dr. Peter Goadsby, Professor of Clinical Neurology at the University College of London, as "probably the worst pain that humans experience." These cluster episodes result from sinus capillaries rapidly cooling and then rewarming, a rebound dilation that sends stinging signals through pain receptors in the neck and head straight to the brain.

Think: a brain freeze that lasts for *hours*. For *days*. More. They can even stay for *years*. Until death do they part.

What this means: getting a brain freeze from hurriedly gulping down a scoop of Clusterfluff ice cream is just a peek, a peck, an unnoticeable blip of that ultimate, unbeatable, unassuageable life-long misery. In comparison to cluster headaches, a brain freeze is the Lilliputian of pain.

The cluster headache's moniker: *suicide headache.*
There is a reason for this.

———

Here are the shrieks that pierce the air. Screeches smack into white walls. Sound multiplying as he can't stop screaming.

First, there's this:

The slight sigh of pain takes shape. Then it transforms into a whimper. Next is the moan. Now a growling groan that gathers in the back of his throat. It cannot be held back. The sound of pain mounting, metastasizing.

The surging, snowballing moan. A moan that doesn't hesitate to be heard.

How it finds its home, writhes throughout our house.

Coils into him.

The source of his pain? Cluster headaches.

Their possible cause? Head injury.

His specific head injury born from an accidental, deadly bump of where skull and metal intersected. All of this and more formed from a right angle that made his life go wrong.

His cluster headaches continue to consume him, and so our skin continues to be penetrated by jarring screams. Our large house is not large enough to house his heinous pain.

Screaming is a symptom of cluster headaches. This, we know.

And the echoes, the unrelenting reverberations. A chill. A shock. Then quivering. Then goosebumps. Hairs stand. Hackles raise. His and mine and Mom's. One body terrorized by cluster headaches, of course. Two bodies terrorized by his wail, the roar that vibrates.

A clusterhead (any clusterhead) (every clusterhead) says there is a pencil in his eye. It pushes itself further in and further in and then some. Forces itself deep into his eye socket, increasing the laceration's size. The pencil feels like a spike, a stake, a poker.

It gets worse. "Red hot," the clusterhead says. A red hot poker and a sharp spike and a splintered pencil all going through his eye. During a cluster headache attack, one eye reddens, wets, weeps, droops, is the nucleus of all that pain.

The clusterhead waits it out. He paces. But even when the pain pauses for a few moments, he is still haunted by the reverberations of its violence, by the knowledge that a cluster will strike again. In eight minutes.

He needs relief. But there isn't anyone who can help him get it. Because there is no cure. There is no one, not one thing that can pick him up and take him elsewhere. To a place without pain. That place doesn't exist. He's stuck. Imprisoned.

A hitchhiker with a hacked-off thumb.

First, she threw away his gun. Then a year later she called the cops—she needed them to storm into his hotel room to stop him from twisting more sheets into rope. Eventually she stopped trying to stop him, stopped trying to redirect his suicidal tendencies. That's when he said he'd fill his pockets with pebbles and walk into the pond behind our house. He never did. My mother told him to go to sleep. The night of pebbles threatened, he momentarily staved off suicide as he abided his wife and retreated to his room.

It is the morning after his pebbles threat that my mother finds him crumpled on the floor, his skin gray, cold.

Suicide headache.

All of this because of a flash of an ill-placed piece of metal slashing into his skin.

There are the images I obsess over. The snapshot of blood trickling down my father's face that shows me when a throbbing misery started to take place. And then there were eight stitches sewn, stitches that fastened his forehead back together.

And yet, there was no healing. No desire for sobriety. No want for life. The only thing in attendance was his continuous hurt.

I blame the right angle that caused the gash, that caused his relapse, that caused his suicide attempts, and then brought on my subsequent abhorrence. I blame it because I don't want to face the explicit spite I had for my father in the first place. Yes, it's easier to blame everything that's not me, because when believed in that way, the hypotheticals won't proceed. How he didn't resist when I pushed him away. How he was never around. Blame justified. An absence only ever filled with howls, the ones that startled me awake.

His cluster headaches were unstoppable.

Eventually, he was unstoppable.

The success of death.

All because of an ill-placed piece of metal.

No one knows what causes cluster headaches.

What we do know is that they are sudden, severe. How an attack lasts for three hours. How they strike at night, strike right as a mind is sinking into sleep, peacefully. Then this: a surge of searing, homicidal pain barges right in. The feel of a skull cracking. Ripped from dreams, jolted awake.

And then it is the next night. And it happens again. And then the next. And then, again.

Clusters are cyclical. Same time. Every night. The zap of an intense pain. The ripped from dreams. This nightmare of these tension headaches, again. Routine.

Circadian.

The Mayo Clinic attempts an explanation:

> The exact cause of cluster headaches is unknown, but abnormalities in the hypothalamus likely play a role. Cluster attacks usually occur within clocklike regularity during a 24-hour day, and the cycle of cluster periods often follows the seasons of the year.

Here lies the hypothalamus.

Size of an almond. Shape of an almond. Not a nut but nuclei-made. *Hypothalamus* means *under*, means *chamber*. It serves a variety of services, such as synthesizing, such as secretion. The hypothalamus stimulates, inhibits, releases hormones—an anatomical character that conducts the story of our bodies, our minds, our moods. In essence—the hypothalamus is the sole supervisor of our cycles.

It controls:
    Temperature
        Hunger
            Thirst
                Fatigue
                    Attachment
                        Circadian rhythms
                            (Cluster headaches?)
                                It links:
                        Nerves to hormones
                    Networks of signals
                Reticular formation
            Breathing
        Sleeping
      And, simply:
    Living

Here lies the hypothalamus.

We don't know what to do with it.

Deep in the center of the brain, a pillow of gray matter surrounds what might be a part of cluster headaches' cause. Scientists, doctors, medical professionals of all kinds try to get to the core of what spurs these tension headaches. They have yet to find it.

The hypothalamus is their only hope.

Even if for just a glimpse of an answer, a blip of a reason.

Time to speak of what they do know:

An attack can last for 90 minutes, and more.

That's the length of 270 successive brain freezes.

That's a hurricane of headaches, and all we want is an answer to *why?*

I see the silver slice of metal.

I see his skin.

I wince.

It is years later.

I remember the silver slice of metal.

I remember his defenseless skin.

I still wince.

There is a cursory remedy.

Pure oxygen.

Pure oxygen disperses the clusters. An evaporation. Just a tidbit of relief.

But then they furl back together. Tight. Tighter. More clusters crack through the skull.

Tubes up a nose that's part of a face stricken with desperation. The attempt to pause what terrorizes. Breathing oxygen becomes a talent, an answer.

Clusterheads plead to whatever god they believe in to never again have use for the word *misery*. To chuck the agony away and pray it doesn't boomerang.

And so they grab their green tanks.

They breathe.

But it's all just a tease.

Here you go. Have this relief.

Just kidding.

The cacophony of clusters re-crashes in.

Again.

And again.

And then tubes are desperately re-shoved into nostrils. And then the pacing re-begins, an oxygen tank pulled along this time. The path in the carpet becomes more defined.

⊢————————⊣

There are a few different types of memory:

Flashbulb

Short-term

Long-term

This is what I remember:

His dead body on a table, scabs on his temples from trying to rub away the clustered pain, the pain that clung to him, that incited his skin to become cold, death-hued. Expired.

Flashbulb: The flash of an unforgettable moment. Sitting in my truck, punching the passenger side seat when Mom tells me on the phone Dad's dead.

Short-term: Temporary memories. Whether or not we finished piling the wood wasn't important enough for me to remember. That's not what this is about.

Long-term: I will never escape these memories. Him, in his bathroom on the other side of my bedroom wall, howling through his pain. My ceiling and walls are covered in glow-in-the-dark stars, coaxing me to momentarily believe I am somewhere other than here. Somewhere safe, special, celestial. And then he yawps again, and I'm ripped from that feeling. I will never forget this moment.

Our brain is physically altered by the experiences we have. As we continue to live, different pathways to our histories continue to be trampled on, packed down, creating a permanent trail on which we can pace around our pasts. When we recall our memories, we re-fire the same neural pathways to get to the origins of the sense of that memory. How the smell of Diet Sprite will fizz into my nose and bring back memories of the empty cans he used to fill with vodka, the plan to be sneaky unsuccessful. And how his brain had its own path. How his hand kept returning to the bottle. A mindless motion. The circumstance of many disorders clustered inside him.

And his rituals to stop the cluster headache pain terrified me. His pacing, his shouting. Oxygen tanks tugged around by a middle-aged man. So much pain I never wanted to witness.

But I witnessed it from the very beginning.

The moment of the ghastly gash, sliced skin. The blood wept back then, then ten years later I wept over him, stood next to his dead body.

Memories.

Groans. Sheets twisted tight to make a noose. Somewhere, a gun.

Now, I pace the maze of my mind. Back and forth and up and down. I have yet to find a way out. I am stuck. Tied. Helpless. Hopeless.

Pounding recollections.

The trampled path of these memories.

I pace.

THEN SHE FLEW AWAY

The problem with dying in private is that the rest of us don't get to watch it happen, and things that happen without us seem less real, not quite finished, maybe even impossible.
—Sarah Manguso

She climbed the stairs. She found her ledge, that hiding spot. That safety. She sat down not knowing what to do next, but preparing for something. Considering. Brain space tangled up in the logic of if she should do this. She was no longer safe in her life, could no longer find that sense of solace.

She walked up five flights to find it.

Sofie's journal lies in front of me, looking up, expectantly, asking if I really want to do this. I do want to do this. At least I think I do. I think so. Maybe. So. Journal opened. There, right there. A phrase inked into the inside cover of that new journal, the one I bought her, a tool to help extract the toxins rooted deep. So severely internal. Eternal.

Her inscription:

Last night I watched myself sleep then I flew away.

Does her journal speak truth? Did Sofie really witness herself sleep then fly? A soothing dream remembered? Though maybe it's a lyric to a favorite song. Or poem. I could look this up, could scour the Internet to find my answer. But I resist, do not want to research it. I want to hope, need to believe that the beauty of those words came from her. That something inside her spoke serenity, could compose such tranquility.

My job was to just be there. "There" being a transitional residency for homeless youth with drug addiction and mental illness issues. I worked overnights, was there for the youth to come and talk to if there was something they needed to talk about. No professional license here, no MSW or LPC or LMSW or LMHC or PhD or MD or any of those letters that say you can help someone. I was just a woman with a sober heart, with a steady and medicated brain, with a belief in each youth's sobriety, there to help them talk through their issues instead of shooting them up or glugging them down or inhaling with a hope that it would all just dissipate, like smoke.

Last night I watched myself sleep then I flew away.

Reading Sofie's journal cleaves me. The pages break into a shattered mind, fracture the rhythm of my heart trying to beat beyond the bottomless canyons of *why?* Because grief is a continuous echo.

A ritual:

Apartment 302. Top floor. Corner unit. The one with bookcases and Christmas lights and thumbtacked images ripped from magazines—the constantly growing collages of angry rappers and tortured rock stars covering thin putty walls. After meds, past 10:00 p.m., Sofie was always a lump on her bed. I saw her sleeping so many times, woke her up so many times to check her sobriety. The breathalyzer putting booze in check.

Memories of standing above her, briefly watching her sleep—heavily—before I reached down and tapped her shoulder. Her resting place just a mattress and box spring slapped on the floor. Clothes scattered about—a symptom of her depression. Each night she was a body of melancholy crashed on a bed, a body that slowly rolled back over, away from me, after blowing a sober breath. Each night I blew out the black candles flickering on her floor as I left.

I didn't see Sofie fly. Though at times she appears in my dreams. I fall asleep and can see, no, *feel* her fly, can breathe in the beauty of that illusion, that image of a soft escape.

Because gravity pushed her down five stories, crashed her onto the ground.

But in my dreams, she flew.

⊢——————————————⊣

In *The Guardians*, Sarah Manguso writes about her best friend who escaped from a psych ward, and ten hours later, threw himself in front of a train. As she grapples with how to understand and accept this event, she meditates on death and suicide, writes to figure out how to tell the story of her dead best friend. But, she discovers, "My friend died—that isn't a story."

There is no plot here. Just a woman, falling.

———————————————

In the video I made to document the weekend I took Sofie and three other youth on a writing retreat in the mountains, I asked the group what they learned most about themselves while there. After a few silent seconds, Sofie slips her low voice into the air, attempts to put words to her experience: "Well, I learned that . . ." a pause, thoughts congregating, body leaning forward over the table, a heavy exhalation, chin palmed, "well . . ." she leans in further, fingers caressing the plump curve of her pale cheek, "I know this is going to be really shallow but," and now she's staring into the camera, eyes piercing past the black jagged line of her bangs, and then she admits, "I love napping."

Removed from the regular routine of therapy appointments and AA meetings and group therapy and psychiatry appointments and case management meetings and job searching and resume making and constantly shaming herself for sleeping too much, for stuffing sighs into her gray apartment instead of going outside like her friends do with their free time, it is in the Colorado Rockies that Sofie owns it. Knows it. Accepts the symptoms of her depression. Because, yes, Sofie slept.

She missed the town outing. She missed the homemade fudge from the general store, missed picking out a small gift—the souvenirs I bought each of them to commemorate our writing weekend.

I blame the unrelenting depression. The illness that trapped her in bed, the sheets a straitjacket that kept her from moving, from getting up.

Sofie slept.

I've been there. I've known that straitjacket. I, too, have slept that type of sleep.

At 10,000 feet up in the air, Sofie sighed—heavily—sank her body into bed.

What dreams can you have when you're depressed? Dreams of sleeping more, I guess. Dreams of a blank slate, I suppose. Dreams that sooth you into that place where you can just exist, where there's no anxiety about how to continue to live. Dreams full of never waking up.

I, too, have dreamt.

⊢————————————⊣

I told her mothers my story, showed them how I connected with Sofie. The psych wards and cutting. Alcohol and mental illness. Risky behavior. Stuck in the belief that it will never get better. Suicide ideation.

A few days after Sofie's memorial service, I went out for coffee with her mothers. This was when I told them my story. This was when they asked what helped me get through the addiction and the mental illness and the body hatred. "What should we have done differently for our sweet Sofie?"

They assumed that because I was alive, I knew the answer.

I wanted to tell them it doesn't matter now. I wanted to tell them that what I learned won't bring Sofie back. I wanted to tell them that no matter what they did, what I did, what we all did, Sofie still would have relapsed, would have found that parking garage, that tall ledge when she felt like she needed it, regardless. That space of flying—no matter how brief her final descent—is what she wanted, was searching for. Flying can set you free. And nothing can ease the gravity, the pain of a daughter now dead.

"You did everything you could," I said.

"I don't want to admit that I couldn't have saved Harris from his death, that I'm not magic, that I'm not special, that I won't be able to save anyone."

And *I* don't want to admit that Manguso's words thrum within me, that I know that fallacy, that magical thinking that says I'm special, that I could have saved Sofie.

Scene: Sofie's bedroom. Her on the bed. Me making a space on her floor, piling the clothes elsewhere, the mess that depression makes in your home. It consumes the concept of cleanliness, sloths you. Unable to pick anything up, because the depression is tiring, tying you down.

This is a conversation Sofie would only have with me.

"Your friends told me you've been cutting."

"Yeah." Her dark eyes dart into mine.

I start with the logistical questions.

"Do you need stitches?"

"No."

"Is anything infected?"

"No."

This next one is most important, as it helps to take away the anxiety about being judged and recognizes we can, in some way, take care of ourselves.

"Do you need more Band-Aids?"

"No. Well. Yeah."

Four years ago my first aid kit was quite impressive. All of the gauze and tape nurses gave me after giving me stitches. A stockpile of tools used to protect what's in from the harsh elements of what's out.

I think back to my cutting days and remember the one question that made me feel better, relieved. A huge exhale.

"Do you want to show me?"

No hesitation. Pant leg pulled up. I, too, used to cut on my legs when I ran out of space on my arms.

She rips off the Band-Aids. My eyes settle with hers on the cuts. They're not that deep, just lines that scratch the surface of trying to attend to what's inside, what torments her. But I know the significance of shallow scrapes. She's not done cutting yet.

⊢————————————————⊣

Manguso writes, "When a poet ends her life, ghouls send lines of the dead woman's poems back and forth all day." We want to find something. We want to know. We want to look at what's left of the one who left us, want to make sense of all this senselessness. We want evidence. To prove we couldn't prevent it. "Or maybe," Manguso says, "we want to find a clue we should have noticed, since it was right there in her poems, all along, that we should have known to save her, that she would have wanted us to."

⊢————————————————⊣

June 28, 2014: Sofie wrote in her notebook how her addiction was gnawing on her, how her desire to stay sober kept yanking on her, like a child wanting attention. She edited this entry, though, as one sentence lives in the margins, perpendicular to the rest of the text. A second thought of just five words: *Its child smile is gone.* Her sobriety was getting frail.

More about addiction:

Fangs grow and drip with sabotage.

Eleven months after this entry, seven months after her death, I dive into her words, her journal, try to understand her and why she wanted to die, but I begin to drown. The handwriting on the page morphs into an image of her face. She stares up at me, the visage swallowing the letters, written meaning transforming, then soaking into that skin I will never see again.

A child's smile is gone.

Sunday night a young woman I worked with was raped. I assured myself that I wouldn't place blame on myself for its occurrence. That didn't work. I blamed myself for not helping her, for not letting her come back to the apartments because she was drunk. She was drunk and at a house full of high people she didn't know, people who raped her. I didn't let her come home. I heard about the rape the next morning. Monday night she returned to the residency. We sobbed together. Hugged. Tuesday night I didn't go to work. Things still felt hard. The rape. Wednesday morning I was scheduled to meet up with my supervisor to check in about my emotions.

An hour before the meeting, a knock on my door. I open it. My supervisor and the Deputy Director of the organization I work for are standing in my doorway.

Something happened last night.

Tuesday night I had gotten a call. Someone had relapsed. Sofie, again. She had been having a tough time. I asked my coworker if I should call her. He said he didn't care. He thought Sofie should be kicked out for another relapse.

It was a Tuesday night when I called Sofie, when she didn't answer my call. I didn't know it was because of a fall. I left Sofie a message, but by then her body had already crashed onto, cracked all over the concrete.

In the 2011 film *Insidious*, the character Dalton Lambert says, "Last night I watched myself sleep then I flew away."

├────────────────────┤

Sofie was nineteen when she died drunk. Who bought Sofie the booze? It's just one of many questions regarding the details of that night I'll never know. How did Sofie get across town? Why was she in that parking garage? Where did the person who bought her the booze go as Sofie climbed up five flights? What did she do for those few hours between when she left after lunch to when she went down with the sun at dusk?

Who bought Sofie the booze?

Some guy, her friends assumed. A guy she was pining away for. A guy who either treated her terribly—which made her hate herself, or a guy who treated her perfectly—which made her hate herself.

Sofie hated herself. So Sofie got drunk. And answers won't un-dead her. But the question nags. We want information. Facts we can grasp. We need to know who to accuse so we can stop blaming ourselves.

├────────────────────┤

Manguso will always wonder what nurse let her friend Harris leave the hospital. "Think about the person who opened the door for my dead friend. Imagine her closing it behind him." And while she knows there must have been more than one nurse there, knows she should assume there were multiple staff members on the ward when someone opened a door, she also knows how "it feels very good to focus my attention on some imaginary wicked, murdering angel."

There is only one place we can go for absolute solitude—inward.

The safe space. Until it's not, and we try to find somewhere physical to go, somewhere to hide from the world. Ourselves. Because no one feels safe when everything feels so exposed. The rawness of vulnerability, that tenderness. The infection of depression. Take off the bandage. Let the wound air out.

She climbed the stairs. She found her ledge, that hiding spot. That safety. She sat down not knowing what to do next, but preparing for something. Considering. Brain space tangled up in the logic of if she should do this. She was no longer safe in her life, could no longer find that sense of solace.

She walked up five flights to find it.

And then the story changes.

Sofie thought no one could see her, thought that the railing she climbed up then over to get down to that ledge was concealed. It was, but not totally. Security cameras caught it all.

They saw her climb down. Though they didn't see her once she sat on the ledge and continued to drink. They didn't see her talk to her best friend on the phone. They didn't see the change in Sofie's face when she agreed with her best friend, when she was finally convinced to not jump.

What they saw was Sofie's first actions after making that decision. She stood up, her body then appearing on the cameras. What they saw was a woman climbing back up and over to safety.

What they saw was her foot slip.

What they saw was how she tried to hold on. How she dangled. How she screamed. How she lost her grip. The security cameras didn't catch the entire fall. A different camera picked up what happened on the ground. The fallen body. The best friend that ran up right then, racing up a few seconds too late, sprinting to the spot where Sofie landed, laid dead.

Manguso: "I used to believe that death would come when I was ready to walk through the last door. When I was done with suffering, I'd just open the door and walk through it." I know that door. I, too, have reached out for it. I've been in that place where I was ready to walk through it, but Manguso twists the certainty of how we come to death, how death comes to us: "Now I believe that someone or something else will open the door."

Gravity is something I can't control.

├─────────────────────────┤

Before Sofie turned away from suicide, she posted a picture
of herself on Instagram. Eyes closed. A slight smile. The ac-
companying text: *I'm finally free.*

├─────────────────────────┤

They held her signature on their faces. Painted Sofie's art on
their lips and eyelids. Long, mascara-ed lashes stretching out
to connect. Memorialize. Black eyeshadow and thick red lips.
Sofie's signature style.

They used her makeup.

To feel a connection. To stay together at the memorial service to show their love for the woman who no longer lives. That
friend. That soul and feel and look of her kept in their memories, shown to the world.

Sofie would have loved that. Sofie would have thought that
was *the shit*. Her lipsticked lips would have opened up, all rise,
would have let that laugh out. They hoped she saw them in the
pews. Hoped she saw how much they cared. Prayed their style
gave her a smile she could keep this time.

├─────────────────────────┤

I saw her a week after she died. Saw her outside. Saw her not
quite hovering, and not in any way floating or levitating. She
was looming. Just outside my sliding glass door, just a few feet
away. The startle, then the jolt of my body that could feel her

there. Right there. Sofie. I saw her standing on my balcony, not expecting to be let in, but just letting me know she's there.

She's here. She breathes lighter now, I imagine. So much more space to move since the straitjacket of depression was unfastened. Uplifted.

Her flight to freedom.

Manguso saves me. "I'm comforted when I remember that energy that appears missing has just gone somewhere else, has been surrendered to the system of the world."

I have a picture sitting on my desk of Sofie and me. It's from when I took her on that writing retreat and she accepted the beauty of sleep. I look at her every time I sit down to write. I look at her while I write this. My desk is cluttered, and I have to push some folders and cups out of my way to make space for my notebook. As I nudge a candle with the corner of a book, the picture of Sofie and me topples over and lands on my floor.

"Fuck," I say.

"What?" My husband asks from across the room.

And then before I can stop myself from saying it, before I can stop myself from even thinking it, I say, "Sofie fell again."

BODY OF WORK

INTRODUCTION

We learned this in school. Were force-fed the essay's acceptable appearance, all our thoughts squeezed into five paragraphs. *If/then* statement. If we write within the standardized confines, then we prohibit explorations of an essay's true beauty. We're taught the expected infrastructure. The bare bones of persuasive narrative. Introduce, provide three bodies of proof, conclude. But. Creativity lives in our bones—pulses in the pith of what makes us. How we thrive in a variety of forms. Like our bodies. Life wanting to move away from social conceptions of beauty, away from standardized bodies, size zero, the expected texts of our looks. Like the confines of structured writing. Acceptable language. Graded. The expected looks of our texts. But narratives are alive and moving (the memoir of scars, the poetry of clavicles, our lungs' language). Let's get to the heart of the matter. We could follow the rules of canon, of grammar, of the five-paragraph form, but the parameters of expression take on different shapes. Always have. We could continue to follow rules of restriction, of thin skin, of showing our bones, but the dimensions of our physical forms want more. Different shapes. Always have.

BODY I: WRITING SKELETAL FRACTURES

We press against the tenuous fences between poetry and fiction and nonfiction and humor and critical writing and academic writing and blogging and every other genre that has ever existed, ever, in order to discover how to discuss our lives. Stretch through our porous boundaries of self, of genre, to touch what's on the other side. Hybridize. Here in these in-between spaces, narrative rules no longer apply. Hybrids help. Hybrids show us how to rethink, resist, grow. Regrowth. How to read differently, write inversely, away from the boxes. Writing is alive like a body. Kazim Ali: "The text is a body because it is made of the flesh and breath and blood of a writer. The mind which declares intention is a collecting of senses. And memories. Chemically it is invented in the brain. Thought is matter." No matter how we have been told to write, our writing is a forever growing thing and it can grow away from expectations. Born anew in new forms. Throw the skeletons of standardized writing into the closet and forget about them. Find the key, lock it, then lose it. Ander Monson: outlines, indexes, his periodic snow. Jill Talbot: syllabus. Michelle Morano: Spanish grammar. And more: questionnaires and lists and prosetry and letters and textual adventures. Mathematical problems, even. Lauren Slater: maybe a fake memoir. Sherman Alexie and Tobias Wolff and their autobiographical novels. Jo Ann Beard: braided. John McPhee: woven. Lawrence Sutin's postcards. Sven Birkerts' objects. Renovate self and paint the world with blue. Maggie Nelson. I have an affinity for hermit crabs. Structure courting content, perfectly juxtaposed to make a (w)holy matrimony of form. To disorganize our thoughts, to let the form live as it wants to live. Such as prose poems, lyric essays, mosaic stories, crossword puzzle interviews, poeticized science. Forever restructure the structure. Transform.

BODY II: RESTRUCTURING THE FRACTURED BODY

The head is how we introduce ourselves. Words. Eye contact. A nod of introduction, recognition. What's up? Past the main three segments of our bodies—arms, abdomen, legs—we reach the conclusion that's lying there, right between our legs. Because what will become of us? Come from us? Come out of us? Beginnings and endings can form into unique shapes and values with a personalized purpose (the face, desire), but it's the body that's regulated. Marya Hornbacher says, "We turn skeletons into goddesses." The narrative of normativity. The strive for zero. It's not for nothing, though, as I've been told that a part of joy is sorrow. The almost literally fought-to-the-death zero that eventually (hopefully) goes away, fades. How to allow this? Acceptance of self. Reject the fairy tale of being s(t)ick thin and all those expectations. And how a body can move away from this, can work against it by creating a new text of physical self. Cut up the archetype. Expose the horror story we believe our bodies to be, solve the mystery of how we can fit in this world by simply fitting in with ourselves (acceptance, yes), and get real here—get a thrill out of living creative-nonfictionally. This is my body. Fact. This is what it says. *Create.* Crack open the zero-shaped shell of social constructions and find the self, the comfortable body that lives within. Powerful. Lia Purpura observes, "How easily the body opens." Coax yourself out. Forget creams and shampoos and toners and diet foods and magic pills and lose ten pounds in seven days. Instead, open up to personhood, to that aliveness. Create. Describe. Feel real with yourself, in yourself and tell the world a new body narrative. Phillip Lopate claims, "When I write, I almost feel that they, and not my intellect, are the clever progenitors of the text. Whatever narcissism, fetishism, and proud sense of masculinity I possess about my body must begin and end with my fingers." The story of subversion. Rewriting the scripts of our skin.

BODY III: BODIES OF WRITING MADE BY WRITING BODIES

Arianne Zwartjes ignores science writing, ignores lab reports with her lyrical explorations of the body. "Our bones surge and flow with blood. Not only a clothes hanger for skin and organs—they are very much alive, vitally interconnected tissue." Hypothesis: If we use metaphors in science writing, then our body of work becomes alive. Because when the norm continues to fester in our physical selves (you must look like this, act like this, breathe like this, *be* this) our bones fuse with fright, become restricted by thematic hesitations of *I'm not doing this right and I never will.* Self-declared failure. Now, work against this. Push your writing into something else. Past the page, past the pessimistic perspective of your physique. Breakaway. Listen for the real stories of your body. They're hidden within the expectations. Un-five paragraph your writing.

See?

Now we're more than what's expected. More than what we're instructed to do—conform to the insistence on the five-paragraph form no more.

I un-social-standard-of-beauty my body. Dreadlocks. Hairy legs. Armpits, too. And my skin that is no longer thin. I'm learning how to rewrite my letter of acceptance. To encourage before criticizing. And end each thought with a *you're doing great* and a *just keep going*. There's always more to write. Always. More to read. Always. Now consider the new shapes of text. The new ways we can read our bodies. Edit. Revolt.

Don't let five paragraphs constrict nor conduct you.

Make anew.

CONCLUSION

In conclusion, language and bodies can be fluid if we encourage them to be so. Because if we write within the standardized confines, then we prohibit explorations of an essay's true beauty. Our true beauty. We're taught an expected infrastructure. The bare bones of persuasive narrative. The methods of storytelling we live by—those that must be complete. Are complete. Inherently. According to Zwartjes: "We live by story and dying without story seems the most terrifying of ends." The terrifying end reached by not writing past oppressive narratives. Move away from it by moving about, by believing in the power of motion, the concept of uncertain future. Believe and keep the body talking. Its strength should never be silenced. Likewise, let's keep the essay moving, shifting. There is no such thing as a final draft. The bodies of (emotionally) provoking books. Stories of skin. Persuade and remake, reframe five paragraphs of an essay that just want to explore. Stretch. To have room to flesh out. We hold spines in our hands as we journey through each page. We hold our bodies in the hands of our perspectives when we read not just the skin, but everything within—the narrative of who we are. Who we might be. Time to read.

Our bodies—this page.

OUTLINE FOR CHANGE

• Lift with your legs, not with your back.

• On the count of three.
    ◦ One.
        ▸ Two.
            ▹ Three.

Problem: I don't know how to start this, how to get things moving.

It's all a bit out of focus.

I need to outline an answer to a complicated question so I can solve it, but everything is a blur.

A black blur.

A blur of black pajamas, actually.

Sweatpants and a sweatshirt, specifically.

His uniform of sorts. The clothes he *lived* in even though he never felt like *living*.

(How to tell the story about a man who no longer wanted one?)

The dad-blur smeared down the hallway in a hasty desperation to go somewhere specific. I sat on the couch, five years shy of being able to buy my own booze, and glanced up as the rushed image of an alcoholic father tried to look cool, look casual, look as if he wasn't blitzing. Briefcase in hand. Excuse flung over his shoulder.

"Gotta go pick some papers up from the office, Chels!"

Let's pause here for just a second and look at 20 key specifics of this situation.

1. Dad's a salesman for Dell.
2. His hours are the predictable businessman-appointed work hours.
3. M–F.
4. 9–5.
5. Today is Sunday.
6. Point #5 points to the fact that the office is closed.
7. Locked.
8. Unmistakably.
9. Though if, by chance, the building was unlocked, there's still that pesky detail of Dad's sloppy uniform that looks even more shit-faced than he is about to be.
10. Because of course this little pajama-outfitted escapade, this lie-filled field trip to a locked office really, truly has nothing to do with the liquor store stationed two miles away from the alcoholic's current location.
11. Briefcase in hand.
12. Note: Dad was sober for 13 years, but decided against that way of living when his ego got bruised in 1999 from not getting a promotion he never

thought he might not get. So, post-no-promo, Dad decided to re-say hello to liquor. From that first re-union with vodka in 1999, to that November morning in 2004 when he died from too much vodka, like any outstanding alcoholic my dad didn't timidly return to drinking. He got drunk. A lot. Though swore he would only drink on the weekends, which is a promise he kept if you believe that there are seven weekend days in one week. This is another way of saying that all of Dad's "relapses" between that first relapse in 1999 and that final one in 2004 that led to his death, technically weren't relapses at all. One must quit drinking before one can commit a relapse. You can't fall off a wagon you were never on to begin with. Dad's actions for those five years didn't consist of periods of sobriety punctuated by occasional relapses, rather his behavior could be considered what healthcare professionals refer to as "using."

13. Wearing black sweatpants and a black sweatshirt to the office (even if no one's there and all the doors are locked) does not reflect the expected impeccable appearance of Dell employees as can be seen by their snappy business-casual attire. This violation could result in a written warning, specified as not being compliant with Dell's dress code policy as detailed in the employee handbook (page 84).

14. I know these things.

　　14½. Except for the page number. I made that up.

15. I, too, worked at Dell.
    15½. In the coffee shop. But still.
16. It was mandatory to wear business-casual attire the first four days of each week with the reward of . . .
17. Casual Fridays!
18. Which meant jeans!
19. Not pajamas, though.
20. Fail.

Un-pause scene.

As he blurred by me in the hallway, I could see his ashy ankles and the socklessness of his feet.

Getting some papers?

Seriously?

Here's my surprised face.

Twelve minutes later he re-blurred by me in the opposite direction, beelining to his bedroom with a bulge in the briefcase.

Another note: the distance between the end of our driveway and the Dell parking lot took at least 15 minutes to traverse via car, but only if you hit every green stoplight between here and there—all nine of them.

Fascinating.

- Countdown to end of opening scene.
  - Three.
    - Two.
      - One.

Numerology: *n.* the belief in a (divine) (mystical) (special) relationship between a number and a coinciding event, like how 46 adds up to mean independent. Numerology is a simple way to find what ways we are valuable in certain situations.

Numerology's numerical values:

1. Individual, aggressor, self, leadership, *yang*.
2. Balance, union, receptive, partnership, *yin*.
3. Communication/interaction.
4. Creation.
5. Action, restlessness, life experience.
6. Home/family, responsibility, artistic in nature.
7. Thought/consciousness, spirit.
8. Power/sacrifice.
9. Highest level of change.

The absolutely valued single digits in which we not only believe, but welcome and consider to be words of fate, wisdom, precursors all leading up to life's results, right there in the numbers. Right here as incited by Isopsephy.

Isopsephy: *n.* adding up number values of the letters in a word to form *one* number.

Isopsephy key to the numbers for Numerology:

1 = a, j, s
2 = b, k, t

3 = c, l, u
4 = d, m, v
5 = e, n, w
6 = f, o, x
7 = g, p, y
8 = h, q, z
9 = i, r

Example #1
CHANGE

C = 3
H = 8
A = 1
N = 5
G = 7
E = 5

So:

$3 + 8 + 1 + 5 + 7 + 5 = 29$

And:

$2 + 9 = 11$

Then:

$1 + 1 = 2$

Which means:

2 = Balance

Balance

    1994 Subaru Loyal (green) = $2,000

    1998 Ford Ranger Truck (black) = $8,000

    2001 Dell Inspiron (blue) = $500

    2001–2005 Private University Tuition = $100,000

Total = $110,500

    Cost of being a good parent ≠ $110,500

    Cost of being a good alcoholic = life

    Cost to rectify emotional poverty = one dad

In the end it all balances out.

MITOSIS

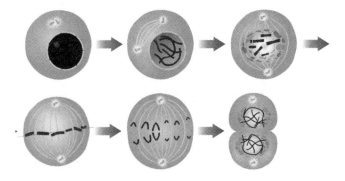

Cells duplicate and split apart. This is called *growth*. Mitosis is simple. A type of duplication. Repetition. Repetition. It repeats itself. Duplicates all of it, everything. After duplication, the two cells split, though nothing of their value is torn. The cleaving makes them self-sufficient. Two identical copies from the original. (You have no choice.) (This is about change.)

Problem: I don't know how to accept, how to forgive him. I have yet to figure out how to cleave my future from his past. I don't know the logistics of *grow*.

INTERPHASE

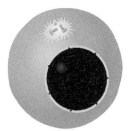

Here is the first phase in mitosis, a resting period between mitotic divisions. In this preparation stage, the cells carry out their normal metabolic activities. The chromosomes aren't identifiable, but are just a loose mass of stretched DNA. This is gestation.

Scene. Texas, 1997: Three years before the blur, two years before the first relapse, I'm fourteen years old and opening my bedroom door. The light from my room casts a soft yellow across the green carpet of the stairs that lead from my door. Four in the morning, getting ready for a softball tournament that starts in a few hours, I head down the dark stairs, and am hit by the large TV screen and its blasting images that set the living room ablaze in its striking, stuttering brightness.

Although it is a huge screen, with my sleep-crusted eyes I can't quite make out what the show is about. It's a close-up of something pumping, some skin working out. I assume it must be an infomercial about a weight-lifting machine. Nothing but muscles could pump that hard. But as my eyes wake up a little bit more, as I rub the crusties away with my pre-teen fists, I realize what I am seeing. A penis pushing into a vagina. It is pushing. And I am watching. I watch, slightly fascinated, slightly disgusted. I should not be watching something like this. I notice the woman's vagina is completely shaved. Shouldn't there be pubic hair down there? I turn my eyes away from the screen, briefly, away from her shaved crotch and the thick, pink, pumping mass, and see a tuft of my father's curly hair sticking up from the peach arm rest of the couch, giving his location away. The pink pumping skin silhouettes his body lying down on the couch. I do not know if he is awake. He's possibly watching, and here I am, also watching. The penis continues to pump silently, as the sound of the TV is turned off. The sex proceeds to no soundtrack.

I saw it. Still see it.

Problem: I don't know how to understand this, my vision of him, blurred.

But before this, before Dell, before he became a blur with a bulging briefcase, he's the VP of Sales at a huge corporation. A decades-loyal employee who worked his way up the totem pole from bottom-level salesman to the VP position, didn't get the promotion nor the raise last week he was certain he would obtain. He's sitting at the desk he's been sitting at for years and will continue to sit at because he failed to get bumped up a notch. There's more going on here than his fissured ego—there's a relentless hurt in his head, as well. Stress and insomnia and diet and genetics all knotted together in his skull, the cluster headaches that throb ferociously each day. The clusters start in his neck, wrench around his temples, stretch down his jaw, then burrow behind his right eye. They're unbearable. So unbearable that he will do everything, do *anything* he has to do in order to relieve the forever echoing ache, the pain that has increased with his career failures, even if that means going against what he has been doing for the past thirteen years: sobriety.

Scene. Texas, 1999: The VP of Sales sits at his desk with his throbbing head. There goes his hand dipping into his briefcase. There go his eyes as they look around the office, hoping no one will glimpse him through the glass window that separates his desk from the other cubicles. There goes his head ducking under the desk. Head tilts back. Swig. And there goes the liquor slipping down his throat. An action that will lead to him being forced to leave his desk. Drunk on the job. A drunk not doing his job. Returning is not and never will be an option.

Gestation: This is called waiting. This is the time period in which we spend most of our lives living. This is another way to say *I survived him.* Survived this, the trajectory of his plummeting story: Thirteen years of sobriety led to four years of using, led to a few honest attempts at rehab and a few bouts of sobriety that never stuck, led to staying in bed, led to hiding from his family as he tried to hide his drinking, and together all of this led to death, led to the discovery of 15 dimes stacked on his dresser that one November morning when I joined my mother at a hospital and kissed his gray, cold forehead goodbye. It was raining outside.

PROPHASE

The beginning of mitosis in which the doubled chromosomes contract and become visible. Two centrioles move to opposite sides of the nucleus. The membrane begins to break down. It is undecided if this is or is not a problem.

Solution: *n.* an answer to a problem.

For example:

- He weighs 252 pounds.
    - ○ Which isn't significant in the sense of trying to point to some numerological meaning of:
        - ‣ his heaviness
        - ‣ or gravity
        - ‣ or the gravity of him
        - ‣ or the gravity of this situation.

- The situation:
    - 252 pounds is the amount of weight that is causing a problem that day.
- That day was:
    - moving day.
    - It was moving day because:
        - After Dad drank himself out of a job, he could not afford the five-bedroom house and so he bought a smaller house and on that day, my parents' possessions were being moved from the big house to the little house.
- On that day:
    - Dad was drunk and Dad was passed out on his bed and Dad wouldn't move and the movers needed him to move so they could move the mattress into the truck because they were movers and that was their job and Dad was passed-out drunk on the bed.
- Dad didn't have a job.
    - He had nothing to do but stay in bed, get drunk, and pass out.
    - Which, on this particular day, created a very inconvenient situation involving 252 pounds of drunk prohibiting four men from doing their job, because:
        - Dad didn't move on moving day.
- Mom then spoke with the movers:
    - Mom: "Can you guys move him?"

○ Movers: "Uh, sure thing, ma'am."

   ‣ The movers made their move towards the heavy, sloshed human on the bed, then said:

      ▷ "What do you want us to do with him ma'am?"

○ Mom: "Just put him on the floor."

   ‣ That's what she said.

   ‣ And then she said it again, only this time with a sigh.

○ Mom (sighing): "Yeah. Just put him on the floor."

• The problem of:

   ○ tangled covers

   ○ a mattress

   ○ 252 pounds of passed-out drunk,

   ○ and 46 square feet of plastic to wrap around the mattress

• is solved when the movers put him on the floor.

• This creates a different problem:

   ○ Mom's desire for a divorce grows.

Example #2
DESIRE

D = 4

E = 5

S = 1

I = 9

R = 9

E = 5

So:
4 + 5 + 1 + 9 + 9 +5 = 33

And:
3 + 3 = 6

Which means:
6 = Home
  = Family
  = Responsibility

And how easy it was for him to finally just drink all of that away. Those terms, that family, his home, that quintessential symptom of alcoholism. His own desire: finish off the bottle instead of pouring it down the drain, keep on drinking because he's no quitter. Plus, he can't figure out how to start over, how to return to sobriety—especially not now. He's too far gone, no longer cares.

The way his alcoholism becomes visible. Glaring. The smell. That look in his eyes. His body too drunk to get out of bed—that's when I quickly shifted away from being a daughter who wanted to love her alcoholic father.

PROMETAPHASE

This is when the bits understand they must move, that what holds it all together begins to unenvelope. Begins to disintegrate. The pull towards the center. Prepare.

Though, by this point there's not much more you can do. The inevitable is unavoidable.

METAPHASE

Gone. Chromosomes line up, nervously. Ready? Here we go.

Example #3

ATTEMPT

A = 1

T = 2

T = 2

E = 5

M = 4

P = 7

T = 2

So:

1 + 2 + 2 + 5 + 4 + 7 + 2 = 23

And:

    2 + 3 = 5

Which means:

    5 = Action

Gun. Until Mom sold it. Sheets twisted into rope. Until the cops intervened. The ones I've never been told but can sense their presence. Dad's attempts to do away with his misery were diverse—creative, even. Like that final one when he threatened to put pebbles in his pockets and walk out to the pond. (Senseless. Insane. Yes. He was.) A decade of plans to do away with himself. So many attempts. So many failures. So what's the plan here? What's the exit strategy?

    Because each attempt was unsuccessful

    Until:

- The 0.46 blood-alcohol level cinched it.
    - Tenacious.
        - There were so many failed attempts, but Dad stuck with it, gave it his all, his 110% for each of those practice tests. And then he nailed that final exam!
            - Flying colors.
    - We can all stop worrying.
    - He passed.
        - His angle on life—now different.

Geometry

- The angles of his skeleton.
    - How Mom found the heap of his cold, gray flesh awkwardly angled on the floor.
        - The jut of knees.
        - The jut of his elbows.
            - Gawkily oblique, tilted, skin aslant.
            - Looking like a dead body on a floor.
- There will be two different angles from two different medical professionals who will give their two different two cents on what this final resting position meant (its reason).
    - "Suicide" says the coroner.
    - "Heart failure" says our family practitioner.
    - We'll never know.
    - Does it even matter?
    - Does finding the right angle on the manner, the correct perspective on cause of death even exist?
    - Can charts and graphs and outlines and diagrams help to understand any of this?

ANAPHASE

Chromosomes separate. They begin to pull away.

Separation. A migration. He went away. Went underground. Went looking for Hades. Well, not really. He was a Christian man without a church affiliation or a relationship with God, so who knows where it is he thought he would go post-0.46. But he knew what he wanted. Was dead serious about getting it right this time and following through with his plans. Intent. Here is the moment when he finally gave in to that inevitable decision, the separation, the slow migration to death that became a viable, post-livable, final decision.

Question: *n.* a matter of some difficulty; a problem. e.g.:

> **Q:** What is an absolute value?
>
> **A:** A number's distance from zero.
>
> **Q:** How much did you absolutely love your father?
>
> **A:** Zero.
>
> **Q:** What was of absolute value to him?
>
> **A:** Absolut Vodka.
>
> (i.e., His 0.46 relationship with it.)
>
> **Q:** What is that supposed to mean?
>
> **A:** That was his blood-alcohol level as determined by the coroner.
>
> (i.e., 5.75 times the legal liquored-up limit. Absolutely.)

$0.46 = 4 + 6$

So:

$4 + 6 = 10$

Thus:
1 + 0 = 1

And so:
1 = Individual
  = Self
  = Aggressor

(The aggressive individual who took too long to remove himself from the situation.) He was consumed with himself, his failures. So wrapped up in hating himself. Alcohol didn't assuage the situation, but it was an effective escape. Liquor swinging this suicidal individual into the cyclical fallacy that getting drunk makes him happy, that escaping makes it better.

Insane: *adj.* mentally unsound or deranged.

Such as
      doing the same thing over and over
          and over
             and over
                and over
                   and over
                      again
               expecting
         different
      results
    each time.
So many effects of how this is true.

One drink is too much and **1,000** is never enough.

$1 + 0 + 0 + 0 = 1$

Aggressor. Individual. Self.

The strength of this breaks through.

Eventually, a breakthrough.

His ending is due to his own breakage.

And how he never spent that $1.50 found on his dresser.

Those 15 dimes stacked up, wanting to work, to be useful.

Everyone just wants a purpose.

The 15 dimes didn't move, though.

Neither did he.

Not after he just hit the floor, again.

Finis.

Finally.

Fact: The covering of addictions through that successful businessman ideal image (polished shoes, stellar eye contact, firm handshake, classy ties, creased pants, crisp collared shirts), the surface level that lied about his sobriety disappeared. Broke. Faded away. Disintegrated. All that was left to see in that phase, was that final way of thinking. Some facts were about to fully come out. The end is unavoidable.

Example #4

FACT

F = 6

A = 1

C = 3

T = 2

So:
6 + 1 + 3 + 2 = 12

And:
1 + 2 = 3

Which means:
3 = Communication

A phone call made on November 13, 2004 conveys 10 essential facts about communication.

Fact: Kate's got a seven-month-old fetus in her belly.
  • Her whole body jiggles as she rightfully laughs. She's on the phone. Dad's being ridiculous. He's having a hard time being clear, communicating what is going on with his life in that moment.

Fact: He's drunk.
  • Yes, Mom had to leave Houston a day early, had to cut short her time with pregnant Kate and just-shy-of three Dylan to get home to attend to the drunk husband/father. She was only going to be away from him for four days. She thought he could stay sober for those three nights, for those four days.

Fact: Nope.

Fact: He calls Mom and is:

- mumbling/slurring/stumbling around some drunk words:
  - "Christ I hate my life
    and I want to die
    and the dog ate my glasses, again."
- Mom cuts off his slurring:
  - "What's that? Pearl ate your glasses, again?"
- Dad slurs:
  - "Yeah. I can't see."
    - Plus he's drunk,
    - has been drunk
    - for the past three days
    - and that doesn't help
      - to clear things up,
      - to clear up his eyesight,
      - in any way.

Fact: Mom leaves Houston in a rush.

Fact: Mom's drunk husband and angry younger daughter are in Austin and so Mom doesn't want to leave Houston at all.

Fact: She doesn't want to take care of her drunk husband.

Fact: Once she leaves, Kate calls him.

Fact: Now, Kate can't stop laughing while he's crying about the slurry lines of his life, because she's laughing about the dog chewing up his glasses, again, which eventually gets the drunk dad to start laughing and they are both laughing now and now Kate's crying because she's laughing so hard and the drunk dad chuckles and her pregnant belly jiggles and Dylan asks Mom *what's so funny* and the father-daughter pair hang up the phone with one more laugh and Kate puts Dylan to bed and nine hours later her drunk dad is dead. Mom finds his gray body on the floor. She tries CPR. Pushes her small palms on his lifeless sternum. Ribs crack.

Fact: The effects of these 10 facts: A doctor and a coroner will make many phone calls to one another, each trying to communicate an opinion on the meaning of 0.46 and 15 dimes.

TELOPHASE

Two distinct membranes develop. Two identical sets of chromosomes are established. Everything divides. The membrane pinches. Mitosis is a cellular calculation, an even distribution.

Calculation
- Let's apply some math from November 13, 2004.
- The number of 2 oz glugs that got him so far gone.

- ○ First there was the 1 that turned into the 2.
- ○ Then there was the 2 that turned into the 3.
- ○ Then there was the 3 that turned into the 4.
    - ‣ Then I could repeat this pattern some more until I reached the exact number of drinks his lips reached out for that final, fatal time.
        - ▷ (i.e., 19.)
    - ‣ But that pattern would get annoying and frustrating to read and I don't want to push you away with annoyance and frustration, because I am, after all, trying my hardest to never be like my father.
        - ▷ So:
            - • Then there was the 4 that turned into the 5.
            - • . . .
            - • Then there was the 18 that turned into the 19.
- • When applied to a situation, one can see that simple addition has the potential to be quite powerful, to carry much significance. Such as:
    - ○ at drink 18 he thought,
        - ‣ *just one more.*
- • His *just one more* is what created a killer calculation, what brought him to that monumental 0.46.
    - ○ The 19th drink floored him.
    - ○ It just put him on the floor.
        - ‣ He passed out, crashed, landed on the floor, unable to get up for good.

Example #5
  DAD
  D = 4
  A = 1
  D = 4

So:
  4 + 1 + 4 = 9

As discussed earlier:
  9 = the highest level of change

I know the logistics of how he accomplished that highest level of change. I know the biology of the human body, the processes that occur when a toxic amount of alcohol enters into it. The *how* is known, but the logistics of *why?*, of *what were his intentions?* are complexities I have yet to figure out.

Logic: *n.* a particular method of reasoning.
- I'm still trying to figure out his intentions.
    - What he was going to do with those 15 dimes sitting on his dresser?
- I have yet to be successful at figuring this one out.
    - But I'm working on it.
    - Putting order to the swirls of what it was like to have a suicidal father.
    - To find a concrete structure when trying to sort my way through the chaos of living.
- Such as this outline.

- Such as trying to un-mess all of this.
- Trying to clear the clutter that created stacks of
  - one predominating question:
    - What the fuck was wrong with him?
- Does it even make sense to try to make sense of (t)his mess?
  - Yes.
    - Outline the incomprehensible.
      - Shape into the shape of logic.
    - Find science in the madness.
      - Contain the chaos.
    - Get a better angle from which to consider.

Diagram: *n.* a drawing or chart that outlines and explains the certain ordering of elements, such as words in a sentence.

- *The dog chased the rabbit.*
  - (subject, predicate, direct object)

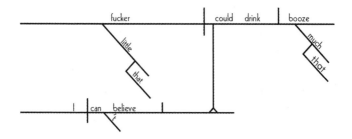

Problem: I don't know how to read all of this.

There's something here about fathers and daughters and liquor and blood and love. Perhaps. Maybe. I hope. I'm sure I had a "pro-dad" phase at some point in my life. Certain that no matter how brief it might have been I must have loved him like a daughter can/does/should love her father. Right? Should shared blood indicate automatic love?

Problem: I intended to write an essay about genetics.

Instead I got this. The outline of a mess I made when all I wanted to do was write a little essay about a well-deserved death.

I wanted to look at genes and heredity, wanted to see what variations there could be in this living organism. This me. Genetics is a field of biology that intersects with the life sciences. The science of being alive. I was curious if in some way I could make science intersect with story and emotion, if I could come up with some sort of system to number, to order, to understand what I've never been able to comprehend—him. Us.

Genetics works in a combination of environment and experience. Nature versus nurture. The alcoholic switch I'm unable to turn off, yet am still curious about how it was first flipped on—by the nature of my body or by how my body lacked a nurturing father?

How the word *genetics* stems from an Ancient Greek word that means *origin*.

From where we came.

Problem: I don't know how to end this. How to fully separate myself from this complex past.

I guess I'll just keep going.

Because it's hard to stop the blur, the flurry of memories of him. He's smeared all over my mind. Stored in my gray matter. A blur of alcoholic father moments. Bulge in the briefcase. Glasses more bent and fractured than he was. The sight of 15 patient dimes, waiting.

Meaning: The $1.50 in dimes that were found, counted out, on his dresser the morning he died.

- 15 dimes counted out every Sunday morning.
- 15 dimes palmed.
- 15 dimes to exchange for the Sunday paper he buys at the corner store.
- 15 dimes traded for the sense that life is still progressing.
- 15 dimes that proved he wanted to keep his life going, wanted to buy the Sunday paper in the morning.

$15 = 1 + 5 = 6$

6 = Home.

6 = Family

6 = Responsibility

6 = 15 dimes that suggest
he didn't want to die,
didn't want to spend the rest of his life drunk in bed,
didn't want to hide himself from the world.

Dimes symbolic of his desire to live, of how he believed there would be a tomorrow. Who counts change before they kill themselves? They are dimes that directly head towards two unanswerable questions:

1. Intention?
2. Need?

I have been obsessing over those 15 dimes for almost 15 years. I need an exit strategy to escape the deluge of dangerous *What if?'s*, the traffic jam of crashed memories that I hope will one day be cleared. When it does, I'll shift my grieving gears and speed away from uncountable memories.

Now.

Go.

Floor it.

TWENTY-SIX JUNCTURES OF
HOW I AM A PART OF YOU

ACCEPT

Cupped in my hands, sipping on some wakeup warmth, I hold the maroon mug my mother gave me on a day when I didn't want to be me. The feeling I felt a few years ago, every day. Any day. Just yesterday. This moment was nothing new. Scene: at the hot springs, changing into a bikini, I can't bear to look down at my bare body. How each glance along the length of my flesh incites another *no*. *No* because I can't stand this, this sight of my too-big body. How my mother says I'm being silly, says I'm beautiful, and grabs my hand, pulls me out of the dressing room, leads me to the water. Like I'm a child. Like I'm not a twenty-six-year-old woman who can do this on her own. Can face this world. Face herself. I can't. My mother lets go of my hand, enters the water and now here I am, standing at the edge of a hot spring with a shifting sense of no, of yes, of no, of yes, of no really, I can do this. How I then do this—this act of revealing a bashful body. I strip off my towel and quickly slip into the hot water where I can hide my flesh. Water's ensconcing qualities. I unwind. And now it's ninety minutes later, and we've extracted ourselves from the hot springs, and have toweled off, and I'm back to looking away from my body as we get dressed, and now we're in the gift shop just to see what trinkets and tchotchkes they sell as souvenirs. Mom buys something. I don't see what. We exit the gift shop and a few strides later we're in the parking lot, in the car and now I see what that something is. "Here," Mom says. And here Mom is, placing a present in my hands. A maroon mug with a curvy woman on it, dancing. An empowering image. An encouraging visage. Mom wants me to know my beauty, to know my body, to dance and move with the freedom born from body acceptance. And because of this mug, because of this curvy woman, I smile. Now, weeks later, months later, years later, it is this morning, it is any day and every day and daily that both hands hold onto a mug that holds meaning. A sense of empowerment coaxed into existence by a mother's gift. As in, I accepted the present back then, and have since worked on the act of body acceptance. Have started to dance often, stoking that feel of freedom. Here she is. Here is the woman I have become. Here I am. Alive. Because there are women who not only brought me here, but showed me reasons to stay. Women who made the earth more inviting than the sky.

BIRTH

Dr. White stands around, yawning, wondering when he will finally get to go home. It's been a slow, snowy day. The world outside accumulating a blizzard-full of white. This woman has been in labor for just a few hours, but his patience is waning. It's his last job of the day—a mother waiting and her birth-resistant baby wading within her. *Come on already,* she silently urges. *You're taking too long. What are you doing in there? Do I have to count to three?* And then Mom pushes and I crown and then the doctor's bored hands birth me. 4:17 a.m., Easter Sunday. Thank god. Finally.

CHI

The flat iron called *Chi,* found in a florescent-lit chain drug-store, aisle three. Purchased by three different women, all related. Taken home to three different houses. Plugged in and sitting on three different bathroom counters. Three Chi's heating up, preparing to be put to use. Three generations of fierce women who refuse to be tamed, who, by the three different colors of their vaguely wavy manes, do not look related, but when at home and they take the flat iron and use it to coax their undulating strands into soft streaks and when the heat from the Chi accidentally meets skin and *sizzle* it bleeds, bubbles, blisters and forms a scab containing bits of a specific protein sequence that says yes, I am a part of you.

DUCT TAPE

A different type of family. One created, made from devotion to the idea of freedom, of *yes.* Duct-taped *x*'s crossing over nipples. Topless women. Bare-chested queers. Cover the female nipples or risk getting a ticket. But it's hot and this is Dyke March and so of course clothes are coming off and the duct tape stays on. *X*'s mark what's perfectly clear: how very queer. Queer as in having names like Pidge and Froi and Trouble and Nern. Queer like the polyamorous transgen-der man with budding facial hair and pre-surgery voluptuous womanly breasts. We champion his choices, refer to him as *he*. His name is West. Queer like a spectrum of gender identities accessorized by glitter and handkerchiefs hanging out of back pockets. Codes. A black and white checkered hanky: right pocket for bottom, left for top. We honor each person's preference. Queer like unicorn parties where women wear boy-cut undies and plastic horns and threadbare vests. Roof parties. Queer like ecstatic. Like everyone is queering themselves silly. This is family. Take pride. The intersex person nicknamed after a bird some consider to be a rat with wings. Or the bisexual Brazilian transgender woman with a koala bear tattoo climbing up her upper thigh. How queer? Righteously. This is family.

EXHALE

There is the sound of her expression. The struggle between encouragement and concern. Seventeen years ago I read to my mother an essay I wrote about the ways in which I could kill myself. Caught between wanting to whisk me off to the psych ward and wanting to encourage me to express my feelings no matter how dangerous they may be, my mother just sat there, in her chair, staring across the kitchen table at her thirteen-year-old daughter, a suicidal writer. She probably said, "That's really good." She probably said, "You're a great writer." She probably said something about craft instead of content, ignoring my grave words, not quite knowing what to do with them. Her breath held in her chest, captured by fear. At some point, years later, after her daughter survived two suicide attempts and started taking meds, after she finally shifted away from insanity with her sobriety, my mother finally exhaled. Relief. Because that teenage girl grew into this woman who wants to stay.

FRIENDS

Once, when I had friends. (Sad how that half-sentence is true.)

GREAT-GRANDDAUGHTER

The great-granddaughter with more than just a mane of vague waves like all the women in her family—four generations of females with similar hair—gets her overtly curly hair from a dead grandfather. His history of black kinks now blonde on her. But when she's old enough, the Chi she will wield.

HOME

Escaping the feeling of a fractured world. Right now, I'm at my mother's house.

I

In the first draft of whatever this is, I somehow forgot to write a section for "I." I find this significant. I thought I was writing this to remember more of myself. To know more of myself. And yet. Here I am prosing about the women who help me to locate the me inside of me. And yet. I, in a way, neglected to attend to the core of all this prose. That would be me. Where am I?

JAMMIES

Night. Visit to my mother. Her house. Nine years post-a-pro-nounced-dead-father. I forgot to bring my pajamas with me. *Jammies*, as my mother calls them. In the rush away from my loneliness, from my lonesome apartment, from the foreboding feeling of this-isn't-going-to-be-a-good-night, the colorless sunset weeping into my bedroom, and thus the rush to her house in need of something resembling comfort. Yes, in such a rush I forgot to bring a simple something to sleep in. At my mother's house, getting ready to go to sleep with the relief of her presence in the room above me, putting on the jammie pants my mother lends me. Hot pink. How funny. A color so unlike her. So unlike me. A variety of cartoon moose with sunglasses arching over their stout snouts, frolicking around the neon pink fabric. And there are words written in the spaces between each moose. *Don't moose around with me!* I laugh. *Don't moose around with me!* How I want to say that to the penetrating memories of a dead father brought on by a sighing sunset. I slip my body into these hot pink moose jammies, take a picture of myself in the bathroom mirror, a smile unable to contain itself. And, later, when I look at that picture after months of forgetting it exists, I will fall in love with the fact of the jammies. How they will remind me of her, my mother, and how at least one ominous night turned out all right.

KNITTING

The brown yarn woven together then presented to me as an example. A swatch of knitting. I'm watching her movements,

continue to be. The specific protein sequence that connects us, that says I am a part of her. She speaks. Four lines, each containing the word *divine*. I forget the other words until the amen in which we follow her lead, lips un-close, say *A-MEN*, heads un-bow, hands un-clasp and break away from the position we only take once a year. The postulations of prayer. And *amen*'s N sticks in the mouth for just a bit, tasting like peanut butter, like it's hard to release. The *n* stays, lingers, until it is pushed out from being lodged in the space between tongue and roof of mouth to somewhere it is better received. Such as an ear. How do you know God is listening? Or rather, what are you thankful for? Now pass the turkey down to the men. And we ladies begin to serve each other salad, and good Christ this feels like the stereotypical and gag-inducing gender shallowness and socially constructed expectations and a prevalence of the forever dieting female and a stupid horrible *what the hell are we doing just eating salad?* subtext. Into our mouths the tradition of what it means to be female goes. The salad has figs in it. And low-calorie dressing. Dig in. But then Great-granny grabs a roll and slathers butter onto it and the mashed potatoes quickly make their way down the table to her as my mother and aunt and I don't touch them and then she heaps three calorie-heavy mountains onto her large plate. More butter. And gravy, too. Her stomach that says it's okay to eat. She's been alive for eighty-eight years. She knows of these things and knows by now how to treat your body better. Such as unchaining the monster of food restriction from your physical form and allowing it run away, to go out of sight, to never come back here again. Such as accepting her body for what it is. She sits there smiling at all of the food in front of her, sits there looking enlightened. Divine.

NUMBER

Eating Disorder Not Otherwise Specified. EDNOS. DSM 307.50. A number I'm a good fit for. So good that the doctor will give it to me, this diagnosis present. Too many women qualify to be assigned this number. So many of us in this situation. Sitting in the waiting room at the doctor's office, waiting to be weighed, praying for the correct number that proves our capability in this battle against bodies. We wait. Together. Though during the waiting we flit our eyes around the room, compare bodies, ours to each other's, wondering if we're bigger or smaller than the woman seated next to us. A waiting room stuffed with women and anticipation and silent prayers that our number descended since the last time we were here. And the secret desire to have a number so low that we are then assigned a new number: 307.50—the one that officially, diagnosably proves to the world we have won the battle against our bodies. And how without an intervention, we will win the war—a body so small it's gone. We'll be gone. Free from these cumbersome bodies we no longer want to carry around.

OBESE

An obese woman talks to her dog. A rambunctious muscular thing. "I told you you'd do that." She laughs at it. The conversation continues. Dog running in circles around the basketball court because for once the court is not littered with small children bouncing flat rubber balls. "You're having fun, aren't you?" An obese woman talks to her dog. And all the fat-phobic judgments society shoves down my throat come hurtling out. Though I stop them before I can blurt them. Yet I can't believe I'm thinking like this—how she must be so lonely with such an unlovable body. Yes, an obese woman talks to her dog. And I wonder if this is the only conversation she'll have today. I walk by. I do not look at her. I do not wave. I do not say hello. I keep going on my way and hope I never fall wayward from this sick determination to forever be in control of this body. I pray I don't end up like her.

POTATOES, PART II

Once, when I had friends, we women would get together on the day every American is expected to eat a dead bird. To stuff themselves silly with dead-bird stuffing. And more. (And the fact of women and their salads.) We queer female friends forming our own family served ourselves more than just salad. As in, rolls. Mashed potatoes. Tofurky. Pass the butter. More gravy. Also, among the six of us we shared six bottles of Three Buck Chuck. We called this Thankstaking. Amen.

QUARTERS

You. You don't look like him. You don't like him. You the daughter, he the father, and you not knowing how to be his daughter. But there's the fact, again, of more protein sequences that hold meaning. Because you the daughter are a part of him—the dead grandpa, your father. Blood, yes. But not apparent. Because you do not look like him and you did not like him. He knew this, easily surrendered to the truth of it. Though there were the times he tried to be a parent. Why believe this? Because you hold out hope. Because he used to wash your truck for you. A subtle sign of care. Because when he washed your truck for you, he filled it up with gas and he filled up the console with a stack of eighteen quarters. It's all that would fit. Fifty cents short of something feeling complete. Whole. The holes of your relationship. He bought that truck for you, even though you didn't know how to drive it. Stick shift. He would have to teach you. Intentional quality time? You will never know. Regardless, the necessary lessons at the top of the hill. *Now keep her still.* There was something there, idling. The decision to be an involved parent, waiting there, staying still inside him, indecisive, and forever debating if he felt like being a fully devoted father. That he could be something else to his daughter. A mentor, perhaps. A man who could teach her valuable things. There was something there that tried to find a greater meaning than the $1.50 in dimes that would be found five years later counted out on his dresser the morning he died. Suicide? The dimes perhaps about to be put to use to purchase a newspaper. His Sunday ritual. Died before he could do so. 15 dimes worth of signs. And that unanswerable question of his intention, of his desire consumes you, still. And now nine years later, and still. You try to drive away from the memories. Shift gears. Desperate. Peel out. Wheels spinning.

RED

To my sister.

Immediately after the 15 dimes, you and I will disagree about everything. His death, mainly—your grief versus my relief. Daughters with different views. Sisters insisting different causes of death. Regardless of our differing reactions, there's the fact of you and I and what we felt with each other after the fact of him being no longer. Lost. Though we can never really lose each other. We have, in fact, and will always be, in fact, enmeshed by the inner thrust of rushing red, yes, the underlying red. That red. That red that from the outside looks like pipes full of blue. They are not. The red inside filled with similar protein sequences. Linked. How even though we disagree on the meaning of a dead father there is the ratio of how I am a part of you. Of how you are a part of me. Of how we have this *we*.

STRAWBERRIES

My mother's garden in Colorado. Decades ago, when I was only a decade old. How she tried to give me a green thumb, to include me in the joy of gardening, the activity rooted in my matrilineage. Three generations of women who will not be tamed, who like to get their hands dirty. The garden more than a hobby, a lifestyle, a need. A type of creativity. Though there is the problem of deer. Strawberries stolen each year. A blow-up owl on a fence post works for a night. But just one night. The deer quickly realize the owl is unusually patient, how it stays too still for too long, even for an owl. The following dawn, deer, fawn hop over the fence, again. More strawberries stolen. Red ingested. Though they never touch the rhubarb. Those red stalks remain. A pucker of a taste of a memory. The only produce that will be a product of my mother's garden. I will grow up on rhubarb recipes, never able to decide if I like the taste. Then, a decade later, I once had a friend named Pidge who wanted to make a rhubarb pie to take to a unicorn roof party. But Pidge didn't know what rhubarb looked like. I took her to the market and thought of my mother. Memories planted within me. I tend to them.

TEXTURE

Dusk. The final touches of a sky turning orange, the switch to pink, no, now purple. Watch as everything continues to shapeshift, color-shift, bring about that end-of-day hue. No longer colorless. The blurring of bodies, mother and daughter watching the day give way to night. Silence between us. We say everything by saying nothing. We connect with the knowledge that I am a part of her. We are a part of each other. Yes, her support. The woman on my maroon mug. The present she gave me of no really, I *can* do this. Here, now immersed in a midnight blue, the air between us strokes my skin. The texture of what connects us.

UNDERSTANDING

The women in my life. Our stories tucked in tight together. We create an *us*. How together we knead nouns into new meanings, let them settle, bask as we consider ourselves, consider each other, and then put them into action, enliven them into verbs. Have fun with a play-on of words. *Don't moose around with me.* And I ask the women in my life, can I essay you? They encourage me to create, no matter how dangerous my words. Create together, even. How it is we understand each other. How I understand all of what our language can hold, contain. I cocoon into the fact of family and all of its varieties, cocoon into you.

VEER

The first time I kissed my father's forehead was when I was twenty-one and he laid dead on a table before me, the announcement made moments ago that he was too dead to be revived, skin graying, growing cold, no longer slack or wrinkled with worry, but thickening skin settling into the fact of him now gone, succumbed to death, successfully veered away from the direction of living as now he is lying dead on a table, a daughter leaning over him, her affection finally showing. I uncocoon myself towards him, but only momentarily. Now, reverse.

WRITTEN

The stories written on my body. How people try to read them. Though some don't want to know. Some try to avoid staring, but cannot help it. Like looking at cleavage, their eyes linger. Another fact of being female. But more. I know the downward spikes of eyes so well. Then, the look up, the adamant eye contact, the trying not to double-take at what they think they just saw. Lines of scars on her arms. Piled up. No, it can't be. She seems so happy. Such a confident and optimistic woman. She's so accomplished. What does she have to be anxious about, sad about? Another glance at the scars on my arms to try and understand my story and why I wrote it like that. The lines are from a time when my language went missing, when flesh met razor because I couldn't think of any other way to relate my story. What else is there to say? That was four years ago. The scars won't ever fully fade. But now I'm armed with a language that feels right on my skin. Something I want to slip into. I write differently now.

XENOPHOBIA

The take versus the give. We take, you give, if you don't give, we still take and we take everything which includes your lives. Please define *genocide*. Tell me: what are you thankful for? The female friends with whom I celebrated Thankstaking, thankful for each other's company on a day that could be lonely with the reminders of genocide and fractured family and dead fathers and other lost friends. The latter of which I hold the feeling of now. Good women gone. And yet, my story moves on.

YOUTH

Image: a younger version of my uptight aunt let loose at my mother's wedding. The picture of this in my hands is older than I am, and how I'm holding a portrayal of attitude uncoiling, of how my aunt's teeth are clenched on a rose's stem, upturned lips not worried about thorns. Bride in the background. The petals of kin. Blood. Red. All held in her mouth. They are so different, though here in this photo their smiles match for just one day. One photo. That wedding day. And I wonder, when did she let go of the idea of letting go?

ZIPPO

The naked woman's torso has a gun for a head. My hand caresses her breasts, the curve of her ass. Pointy-nippled naked torso. A butane flame sparks out of the revolver where there should be a face. New Year's Eve. 2002. Waco, Texas. The weird vibe of being a drunk surrounded by other drunks I don't know. I'm with my girlfriend wondering if these Wacoans are wanting to kill this shaved-head-woman following around the cropped-short blonde they know—their old friend from high school. I avoid stares, keep my head down as we walk through the living room, past a coffee table composed of a collection of splinters. A jagged pile of objects strewn on its surface. A broken bong lying on its side. A slew of *Hustler* magazines spread out. A zippo lighter. A woman's torso and a gun instead of a head type of lighter. Too completely terrified to even think about these people, about what type of person would want to own that type of Zippo, I follow my girlfriend to the backyard, crowd around the keg of Natty Light, and contemplate how I want to steal what scares me. That lighter. Such extreme misogyny. Yet I'm in love. Such imagination. Admirable innovation. So many ways to hate. I want it, want to hold that type of creativity no matter how offensive it may be. "I'm going to the bathroom," I declare. Girlfriend shrugs. No Wacoan cares. I cross the back-yard, tall weeds crashing into my shins as I walk through them. The screen door snaps my ass as it sharply closes behind me. Now I'm in the living room. There, the lighter still lying amid splintered wood. No one else in the room. Just me and the gun-headed half-woman, now in my pocket. Liberated.

LYING IN THE LYRIC

I know I can make this all poetic and shit, can find some metaphor to wrap this essay up in, like I'm giving you some present with pretty pauses and illuminating illusions. Or, hell, I can wallow in the sorrow of the story that I'm not quite sure I want to tell you yet with some soft, long sounds, avoiding words with *k*, with that hard *c*, sidestepping the cackle of the stark *ch*.

Instead, I can soak in the *l*'s and *s*'s, wind around some *w*'s and give the gust of an *r* or two to reveal the purpose of certain ideas and sentences with more effective emphasis.

Right?

There.

Some one-word paragraphs.

Beautiful.

And here's _____.

An incomplete sentence.

I know the poetic pretense here can proficiently populate the reader's inner parenthesis with some self-deflecting linguistic tricks, can expose myself not through sentiments, but swaying, as in persuading sentences, traversing into the categorical territory of "vulnerable" as I raw myself out with

words such as emotive, mawkish, expostulate, lugubrious—
the ones that are big hits on the GRE vocabulary test.

|———————————————|

Then I can throw in some decorative characters or punctuation or symbols of some sort or whatever to give this essay a
segmented look.

|———————————————|

Now, in this post-uber-lyricized moment, I find that to be a
futile task.

Because there's no lyric or lovely, no poetic way to say I've
been lying to you lately.

|———————————————|

According to its popular-opinioned definition, there shouldn't
be any prescribable form to the lyric essay. That would defeat
the purpose of a lyric essay's elemental and unconventional
innovation. Though I could tell you about the characteristics I
have come across—which may at some point include the term
vulnerable, or more likely *brave*, and how I have started to
despise the exaltation of that latter concept in regards to writing nonfiction. One could say that in order to gain readership,
one could take a traumatic (read: vulnerable) experience and
transform it into a type of art, could dress it up with lyric
language and bring poetry to the pain in order to honor it.

But that's not being vulnerable. That's called being deflective and pretty.

Here, I will begin to address *you*, because you could be the person I'm lying to, and while you most likely are not that person—I am, after all, admitting to a lie and therefore am hoping you don't read this—if you do read this then I'll hope that you, like all you readers, assume I am not addressing *you*, but the general "you" as a literary device to bring you (the reader) more into this confessional essay.

It makes you a part of this.

Part of ~~pain~~ art is sharing.

You'll be more receptive to my lying if I can find a lyrical way to admit all of this. My command of language can bring you into a more conceptual space—how I can distract you with beauty, because what I have to tell you is ugly.

So far, I think this is working.

We are now a third of the way into this essay and all I've really done is make a vague (yet so vulnerable!) admittance that I have been lying to you lately. The subject of said lie is still silent, because I'm still clearing my throat.

And now I'll add in a beautiful quote in order to give you an image not of me doing that thing I'm lying about, but to ricochet away from, to delay my confession.

"I live between mountains and take my smallness, like a pill, upon waking."—Catherine Pierce

The lie is not that I haven't been taking my medication.

The lie is not that I wake up angry each day because I'm still alive.

The lie has nothing to do with my body.

One of these is a lie.

It's time to lay this all out for you, because if I take this any further, the suspense in this essay is going to fizzle.

If it hasn't already started to.

⊢————————————⊣

Elements of a lyric essay: Metaphor. Research. Bullet points. Pace. Poeticism. Odd concepts. Fragments. Surprising verb and/or noun-turned-verb (i.e., a noun verbed). (You can totally Chelsey a sentence.) Surprising structure. Surprising imagery. Unconventional associations. Juxtaposition. A declarative and/or witty and/or telling title. Subtle humor via wordplay. Quirky way of looking at and addressing the theme(s). At least one paragraph so elusive that even the author isn't quite sure of what she's trying to say.

⊢————————————⊣

Mandatory elusive paragraph:

"Lie" is a word of which I've learned how to live, live with. With this word tucked into my pocket—into my little pocket of my lie-filled world—I've created a cornerstone of my life based on living myself into the corner of a liar identity, an identification with (the) (")lying(").

———————

Actually, I'm not certain I'm anti-fizzling. Don't I want all of this to go away? Don't I want to keep up the lie and continue to fade into each day? Don't I want you to think that everything's fine, that of course I've been eating, and so of course isn't it true that I don't want you to discover that lie for as long as I can lay it down in the air between us?

We have arrived at the setup of the lie.

Yes, I've been eating. True story. But at thirty-two years old, I have yet to figure out how not to un-swallow.

Lately, each day, I've been puking.

Always, every second, I've been hating my body.

Shame prompts lies. Everything's fine. Here, look at this beautiful line:

Tell me then what will render the body alive?

That's not actually my line.

It's Jorie Graham's.

But it is my question.

———————

You can't prescribe a lyric essay. There is no take two fragments and call your asterisks in the morning of the next chunk of white space offered. Something just dawned on me. I tell my freelance clients that, when you have no clue what the hell to do next in your essay, or even if you have no idea what the hell you're actually *doing* in an essay, then lyric the shit out of said essay. Get all hybrid-ish with it (which, though phonetically identical, is not the same as a European person under the influence of marijuana, a "high British" person). Scoot yourself into a hermit crab's shell and see if thinking about your vulnerabilities (read: confessed lies) in the form of a job application brings some awesomeness to your essay.

Name: Bulimic.

Previous work history: Clinical Director of the Surplus Food Non-digestion Department.

Education: BA in Sound Muffling.

I could end this on an apology. I could end this with a plea. I'm going to end this quietly, sneaking off to a space where I can be alone and do my thing and hopefully you can't hear me.

This is called muffling. Hushing. The let's-move-on-already-ing.

And now I need a metaphor or a statement that will tie this all together, that will circle back to the beginning, because my life is a cycle (fill empty fill empty fill empty fill), but all I can feel now, post-revealing, is the stark separation of mind and body because of my shame, because of sharing. Now I can only hear the harsh sounds of *k*, of *c*, of *ch*, and even of *q*. I question the chasm created by killer li(n)es.

One should mention *hiding behind form*. Or, not to have every essayist hate me for such a statement, one should instead mention *content shaping into form.* Or, *complex content contemplated through an unconventional structure.*

I must admit, I don't know much about face-to-face confessions. I deal with the world through my words. Though I know that feel of *vulnerability* when letting go, when letting it all out. A laundry-drying cliché of sorts. Though perhaps a more apt word to use in this specific essay is *purge.*

You'll still love me, trust me now that I've told you all of this?

Right?

There.

Some one-word paragraphs used for prevention and protection from facing you.

Beautiful.

And here's _____.

THIS:

A switch in point of view and now I can hide behind you.

You admit a lie. You know you need to stop doing this. You don't know if you're talking about the lying or the puking. You just know you need to stop doing something. You don't know how to stop doing anything. You are addicted to everything. You don't understand how you became such a hot mess, though you wonder if it has anything to do with how you dress the ugly realities of your existence with creative sentences. You refract, though hopefully not repel. You realize every sentence in this paragraph begins with *you.* You know that's not okay. But (!) it works so well to hide in writing, to let the conversation curve around vulnerability and into craft. What a great point of view we have going on here. Let's talk more about that. Let's look at juxtaposition and pacing out a segmented narrative arc.

Let's not analyze my life that lies on the bathroom floor—living, lying fragments.

RE: COLLECTION

It's time. Time to take a wet paper towel to the top of my bookcase. The bookcase that has been sitting here, undusted, for seven months. I've avoided this chore simply because I find it annoying. Having to move all the picture frames, all the favorite books on display, all the knickknacks from inside jokes and miniature mementos just to wipe off a surface that will inevitably get dusty again. Pointless.

However:

Today the bookshelf dust has grabbed my attention. I was looking for my copy of *Bluets* because it's just been one of those days—where chaos keeps on coming, making impacts and rippling out, echoing along with everything else that has gone wrong. Since this is not the first time a single day has felt like one big production of disarray, I know what to do to reset my nerves: ingest 240 doses of Maggie Nelson's poetic exploration of her blue collection. During this search, my eyes eventually drifted up to the top of the bookcase and I saw something that I, for some reason, had yet to notice.

My father's ashes are collecting dust.

There's more to dust than its unpleasant aesthetic. There's some symbolism and metaphors its existence has accumulated. Dust also functions as a measuring mechanism. Its height and density speak to how long something has gone untouched. Understanding the symbolism of dust is easy, but accepting what it actually *is*, what all it is made from, isn't.

Particles in the atmosphere are unavoidable. They're fact. Pollution, soil. The results of an active volcano. The dust that resides in human environments has a variety of ingredients, too. In the home, in the office, in all of those small spaces we've constructed to live and breathe in, the air contains a cocktail of fibers, hair, and minerals from the outside world. Meteorite bits, even. Plus, dead skin cells we shed by the thousands—daily.

Because microscopically speaking, 40,000 deaths happen to each one of us, each day. Layers of us leave, jump ship, fall off, fall down. Which is to say that the particles all around us, the accumulated atmospheric specks that gather and coat our lives, consist of what our bodies leave behind.

When my father died, I surprised myself by keeping parts of the life he left behind. I never thought I'd want a dead man's possessions—especially not from the man whom I saw as the catalyst for every problem in my life. A few weeks after he died, though, I got an inexplicable urge to keep reminders of him—objects that created the story of his life. Sweatshirts. Wallet. Belt buckle. Pen. Even AA coins from his erratic attempts at sobriety. I didn't understand why I wanted mementos, wanted to keep him near me, in my life.

Throughout the nine years after his death, I hauled his favorite sweatshirt and childhood baseball glove around the country with me each time I moved, but I never realized what the impetus was to keep some of his shit. A thought slowly formed and revealed itself through each of those years, and it's what kept me from tossing his objects away. Each memento was part of a story, stories that together created a fuller understanding of my father. Objects as trailheads to some of his tales as told by my family. Like the marble paperweight on my desk. A decade after Dad's death, his own father died from liver cancer. I lived in the same city as our grandfather, but my sister was states away. She and her partner flew in for the funeral and stayed for five days. That first night, while we were all just hanging out and catching up on life, Kate looked at my desk, saw the small slab of polished marble. Regardless that ten years had passed since our own father's death, Kate recognized that squat polished rock, recalled some memories, some impressions of Dad that never existed in my experience of him.

Though the paperweight held little meaning for me, other than the fact that it was his, for my sister it was a memory from the time during that summer when she was sixteen and worked for him. This was when he was sober—those years before the cluster headaches and the depression hit him—and so my sister's stories are about what our father was really like: fun, engaging, playful. Loving. Like what an actual dad can act like. This wasn't the father I had, wasn't the man that I knew—

the one who hermitted himself into his room, crawling into a bottle, furling into a drunken stupor after he was fired.

She told me about his humor and kindness. His appreciation of well-made pens—like the one of his that I have—because he respected his secretary's need for his hand-written directives to be legible. My sister spoke of how he loved us more than he showed. That he, like everyone, was just trying to find a way of life that made him happy. With each recounted story, I stopped considering the objects I saved (read: my dead father's shit) as heavy luggage I hauled from one apartment to the next for reasons I didn't know. Instead, and for the first time, I saw him as a human. Saw his humanness. Saw my father as someone I wanted in my life. Too bad he was dead, but at least I had those two tablespoons of him.

Now, his ashes sit in a wooden box on the top of my bookcase, covered in dust.

Despite my aversion to dusting, when I see the layers of fibers and dead skin cells, I wet a paper towel. It's the symbolism that prompts me. Its meaning of the passage of time, things gone untouched, and the fact that I was surprised by the dust.

I feel a little guilty about all of this—as if I forgot about Dad.

Which I did.

I forgot about Dad.

His ashes.

———

The concept of dust collecting on ashes intrigues me. Dead human skin cells accumulating on dead human body ashes. Fascinating. Mirroring my reaction to dust, I become curious about the story of what's inside that little wooden box—the ashes, their abstraction. What parts of my dad—his body— I now keep near me. This time, my intrigue isn't rooted in symbolism or metaphor. This isn't about religious beliefs or spirituality. It's not about the cost of burial, or where we can go and what we can do to remember our dead.

It's the logistics that interest me.

Specifically, the steps taken to create a certain type of combustion. A vaporization. Oxidation. I'm talking about cremation. All of this in the context of what to do with a dead body. My mother, for instance, shoved Dad's ashes underneath the stairs in her basement. Almost a decade later, we excavated him so I could put Dad in a small wooden box to be closer to him.

Through cremation, the body returns to its basic chemical compounds. Gasses. Ashes. Mineral fragments. This process speaks to the only accurate thing we can do with our dead: figure out what to do with them, where to place what remains.

It begins with nine furnaces, four openings, and a maximum of three normal-sized corpses. Then, 1700 degrees (Fahrenheit) is applied and a half-hour later incineration is complete, the body now back to those basic chemical compounds. Gasses. Ashes. Mineral fragments. Elements that all fell down, eventually burnt out. The body's basics distilled, then collected. However, at this point what's really left are just burnt bone fragments. They are then swept up and tossed into a *Cremulator*—essentially a high-capacity, high-speed blender. Twenty minutes later and you either get four pounds of female ashes, or six pounds of male—both with the zest of other incinerated bodies. As in, an unavoidable consequence of cremation is that minute residue from a previous charred individual remains in the chamber, resists being swept up. Ashes mingle.

Who, I wonder, is my father's urn-mate?

Who, I wonder, is the "I" that coats him?

Which is to wonder which "me"—the despiteful daughter or the understanding women—exists in the dust that his ashes have started to collect.

———

Collect. Accumulate.

Also: Amass. Assemble. Compile.

Cluster. Gather.

Congregate.

Queue.

These are the things I have done, am doing. Voluntarily or not, my cells vault and land on the nearest surface. The dead cells aren't entities I can control. Sure, there's lotion and soap and water and clothes and a number of things that I can use to cover my skin, to keep my epidermis—all of it—with me. Ultimately, though, I don't have a say on the biological ways of my body. Nor the roles that chemistry plays. The performance of genetics. Anatomy has a mind of its own—even breathing is an involuntary process. Blood pumps automatically. Nerves have conversations and never care to enquire about our input. Dead skin cells flake off, flock together, stockpile themselves on my bookshelves, regardless of my desires. Nothing can stop their deaths. Not me. Not even themselves.

Apoptosis is when cells condense, shrivel, fissure, die. Because when cells aren't killed by outside sources—blunt trauma, sharp objects, hot surfaces, and all the possible side effects of having a vulnerable, permeable membrane assigned the task to keep each cell safe from what surrounds it—they die by suicide. Cells are born with the instructions and skillset to create biochemical events that will change them. Morph them.

Cellular suicide.

Billions of cellular self-destruct buttons pushed daily through two different avenues. *Intrinsically*: a cell senses stress, then begins to remove itself. *Extrinsically*: a cell sees how a situation is going to play out, then signals a cell to begin to fissure away.

Biologists call apoptosis a highly regulated and controlled process. That it can't be stopped once it has begun. That some parts of a cellular body will engulf the harmful contents inside itself before they can spill out and cause damage to surrounding cells.

Analogies abound. Intrinsic avenues are used. I've always wondered about what made my father take those final sips, if something in him had been growing since his birth to one day activate his eventual self-made end. Maybe he saw that he was the problem, that he was what was causing his nuclear family stress, and so he took the intrinsic avenue to death.

Or maybe all of this is extrinsic. Yes, genetics, but maybe there was an outside force that signaled him towards suicide. The cluster headaches, the youngest daughter who did nothing to ease his pain. I question what part I played in his death, if I became what activated his internal pre-programed executioner. His life ended when his body could no longer keep him alive, and I can't help but wonder what part my anger towards him might have activated the self-destructive parts of him.

Either way, this is all to say that on the most basic biological level, each cell of our being knows what to do in order to do away with itself—every microscopic part of our living bodies is pre-programmed to self-destruct.

What this means:

Each cell's story concludes with a suicide.

How many stories had my father collected?

I think of his ashes. I think of what's on the small wooden box.

How many of my own stories have collected on top of him?

And which ones?

My dead cells contain their own stories. I've already shed the skin I had when I last talked to my father. We argued about ice cream as I found yet another excuse to yell at him for not caring to know more about me. A week later, when I kissed the forehead of his dead body goodbye, new cells were already growing. Always. Then that skin died, flaked off, and with each regenerated layer of flesh, I continue to grow through my different considerations of him. The layers of me that despised him are gone now, most likely, and what's left are the memories of learning how to let go. And as cells shed, there's an emotional release as well.

Like when I threw my bookcase away. Prior to owning the bookcase that's currently collecting dust, I had one that my father built me before he died. It was a solid one—a bookcase I loved regardless of sentimentality. He built it during the last months of his life, during that one week when he tried to be sober. Replacing alcohol consumption with furniture building, Dad made that bookcase from the materials he bought at the Home Depot down the street. Wood, nails, a hammer, a level, paintbrushes and veneer. He built the bookcase, gave it to me with pride, and I was actually appreciative. Shortly after, though, he returned to drinking, then we fought about ice cream, then he died, and then I kissed his dead forehead goodbye.

There are some of those stories that I shed, like how I would eventually let go of the bookcase he built me. Seven years after his death, I had to move across the country and couldn't afford to haul my stuff with me. I knew I'd have to throw away the bookcase, but I didn't feel like I could. As if releasing the bookcase from my possession meant I'd lose him again. But, as my best friend pointed out: "You won't lose him if you throw the bookcase away. He's already gone. You'll always remember him regardless if you have the bookcase." So I gave the bookcase to a neighbor, let go of that tangible memory, and moved across the country.

Moved on.

This is the stuff that makes dust: dead human skin cells shed, fallen. Billions of them. Piling. A dusty layer of dead human bits. Collecting.

The dust of dead cells that fall off. Like a leaf from a branch, like a father from a family tree. We are pre-programmed to shift into death. To leap, leave.

Because there's the fact of proliferation. The effects of those that should die, but don't. Cells stack up, pile, mountain beyond the limit of our internal rate of removal. This brings our bodies into a cancerous state. And so ironically, beautifully, even, millions of microscopic deaths are what keep us alive.

I'm incapable of ignoring an analogy:

Dad had too much pain, too much sadness. Frustration. Anger. Then alcohol. From this, I became resentful. Spiteful. Cause and effect spreading like cancer. And then he died. And then our relationship got better. Because when closets get cluttered, attics get dusty, basements get stuffed with useless junk, we do some spring cleaning. Get rid of what we don't need, what no longer feels vital.

I remember how one of my childhood chores was to weed the flower garden, to give room for beauty to blossom.

Cellular suicide helps the next generation to grow. Dad did, also.

One bookcase is thrown away. Another is about to be dusted.

Through his death, our bodies have finally grown close to one another. Our story didn't end with his last breath.

These are the layers of meaning I sift through. Sort out to find an answer. I remove the charred bone fragments of memory and blend them into a new, lasting consistency. Because our stories will continue, making new understandings and perspectives—perhaps even analogies. I let the layers of dust settle, because they point to the fact that parts of me have fallen—which is evidence that I'm continuing to live, to create more space for things to grow—like my reactions to how my father's ashes are collecting dust. I take the wet paper towel and start wiping away the deaths that have helped me to move on, to grow.

IN GRATITUDE

Being a book about rhythms and cycles and whatnot, it's only fitting that I started this collection during my first year in the fantastic Rainier Writing Workshop MFA program, and completed the final essay during my last residency. Most of these essays were written during my first year when I was under the encouragement and guidance of the *oh-my-god-that-woman-can-WRITE* essayist and poet, Lia Purpura. Thus, Lia: oh my god, thank you! I also want to thank my second- and third-year mentors who supported me as I finished and revised this collection, Barrie Jean Borich and Dinah Lenney. And a huge head nod goes out to both the founding and current program directors—Stan Rubin, Judith Ktichen (miss you!), and Rick Barot. There are so many great writers associated with RWW that to list them all here would add about another hundred pages or so onto this book. Though listing those names wouldn't be a waste of paper, I'll just give this special thank you to those in the program as a whole: Thank you my RWW tribe!

Next up: family. These are the people with whom I'm swimming in the same genetic pool, as well as the friends who are more like family than buddies. Mindy Clammer, Marya Hornbacher, Kate Buley, Sabrina Long, Pat Hall, Betty Ann Hall, Denna Cannon, Clayton Davis, Bernard Grant, Tammy Robacker, Kristina Moriconi, Kristy Arditti, Emma Patrick, and my awesome nieces and nephew who keep me smiling: Dylan Buley, Maddie Buley, and Lily Buley.

Lit-world-wise, I must thank Keaton Maddox and the Red Hen Press team for believing in this book, the literary journals and their editors who published these essays, and to all of the readers and writers who cheer me on and support my work.

This goes out to those who have left my life, yet their spirits keep me going: Jeffrey Clammer and Sofie Egan. And a big, loving thanks to those who prove the power and strength of community in the face of tragedy: Kelsey Fonzi, Jennifer Rice, Kelsea Weatherly, Shyla Montoya, Kris TJ, Elyse Crowder, Jonathan Sherman, Nathan Sherman, Taylor Bayles, AJ Jamison, Suzanne Kittelson, and Anna Czaja.

Finally—Spencer Darr. Thank you for encouraging me to keep writing through all of those times when I thought, "Fuck this shit. It's too hard."

BIOGRAPHICAL NOTE

Chelsey Clammer is an award-winning essayist who has been published in *The Rumpus*, *Hobart*, *The Normal School*, *McSweeney's Internet Tendency*, and *Black Warrior Review*, among many others. She is the Essays Editor for *The Nervous Breakdown*. Her first collection of essays, *Body-Home*, looks at how we can find the concept of home in our bodies. You can read more of her work at www.chelseyclammer.com.